The Holadays

THE COLORFUL LIFE OF GEORGE MEACHAM HOLADAY

The Holadays

THE COLORFUL LIFE OF GEORGE MEACHAM HOLADAY

by Rachelle L. Tuttle

The Holadays Series

Published by Tallgrass Prairie Books
https://www.tallgrassprairiebooks.com
info@tallgrassprairiebooks.com

Copyright © 2024 Rachelle L. Tuttle

ISBN: 979-8-9905605-7-4
Library of Congress Control Number: 2024913107

Notice: The information in this book is true and complete to the best of our knowledge. It is offered without guarantee on the part of the author or Tallgrass Prairie Books. The author and Tallgrass Prairie Books disclaim all liability in connection with the use of this book.

All Rights Reserved. No part of this book may be reproduced or transmitted in any form whatsoever without prior written permission from the publisher except in the case of brief quotations embodied in critical articles and reviews.

DEDICATION

In loving memory of my beautiful mother, who not only gave me life, but ignited in me a passion for reading and genealogy, profoundly enriching that life. Mom, I think it all started when you read all the Laura Ingalls Wilder books to me. I don't think you ever knew how much I loved snuggling with you as you read aloud.

Until we meet again, my dearest mother.

~

"I am bound to them, though I cannot look into their eyes or hear their voices. I honor their history. I cherish their lives. I will tell their story. I will remember them."

Author unknown

To forget one's ancestors is to be a book without a source, a tree without a root.

Chinese proverb

TABLE OF CONTENTS

Dedication v
Preface ix
1. Background 11
2. Contrary to Discipline 29
3. The "New Lands"– Iowa Territory 33
4. California Gold Rush 53
5. Adair County, Iowa 67
6. Winterset, Madison County, Iowa 79
7. Pike's Peak Gold Rush 87
8. La Paz, Arizona 95
9. Prescott, Arizona 117
10. California 123
11. Death of a Pioneer 133
12. Lydia Hollingsworth Holaday 141
13. George & Lydia's Children 149
14. Mini Biographies of Note 173
15. Descendants of George M. Holaday 191
References 207
Index 211
About The Author & Contact Information 221

PREFACE

In the chronicles of American frontier history, few lives are as paradoxical and compelling as that of George Meacham Holaday. A man of stark contradictions, George began his life in the Quaker faith but soon ventured down a tumultuous path that led him to become a horse thief, squatter, gold rusher and bigamist. His story is one of daring exploits and audacious gambles, a narrative almost lost to the passage of time.

George Meacham Holaday's legacy is as varied as it is extraordinary. He embodied the restless spirit of the West, engaging in diverse enterprises from owning hotels and saloons to fervently trading land. His public roles were equally significant; he served as a sheriff, the first judge of Adair County, Iowa, a member of the first Arizona Territorial Legislature, a justice of the peace and a judge in several locales. Yet, his personal life was marred by scandal—he fathered children out of wedlock and abandoned his family to run off with his mistress.

In this book, my goal is to paint the colorful life of George Meacham Holaday, a man who left an indelible imprint on the early days of Iowa, Arizona and California.

George's story is a window into the complexities and contradictions of the American frontier, a testament to the rugged individualism that shaped a nation. This book will explore the heights of his achievements, as well as the depths of his transgressions.

George Meacham Holaday was nearly the first, if not *the* first Holaday in Iowa Territory. The same can be said for Ezekiel Hollingsworth of the Hollingsworth surname. Between them, there are thousands of descendants.

CHAPTER 1
BACKGROUND

QUAKERS

To fully appreciate George Meacham Holaday and his wife, it's essential to begin with a brief overview of Quakers — their unique belief system and the structure of their meetings. Both George and his wife Lydia descended from long lines of Quaker heritage, deeply influencing their lives.

The Religious Society of Friends, also known as the Quaker Movement, was founded in England in the 17th century by George Fox. Early Quakers, or as they often refer to themselves, "Friends," were persecuted for their beliefs. Among those beliefs were equality of all persons, pacifism and the rejection of religious ceremonies. They believe(d) that God exists in every person, and each individual has a direct connection to God. They rejected social hierarchies and titles, including those associated with traditional forms of religious authority. They refused to pay the mandatory tithe to support the clergy of the Anglican Church. All of this was a massive affront to the Church of England and seen as radical.

They refused to participate in war, violence or oaths, instead advocating for peaceful conflict resolution. They refused to bow or curtsey and did not remove their hats. They were "plain" in language and dress, lived simply, rejecting ostentatious displays of wealth and materialism. They did not gamble, drink alcohol or dance. Various acts were passed that led to persecution and even imprisonment of Quakers in England. Some Quakers fled England for Ireland, where they established themselves in 1654. In 1675, full scale migration to America began. By 1750, the Society of Friends was the third largest denomination in Britain's American colonies.

In America, Quakers would become pioneers in various social justice movements, including abolitionism, women's rights and prison reform. They often helped in the Underground Railroad.

They were meticulous record keepers, maintaining detailed records of their religious and community lives. Among these records were minutes of birth, marriage and death, membership, discipline, financial reports and correspondence. They placed great importance on keeping comprehensive records, which today, are a valuable historical and genealogical resource.

Quakers attended various types of meetings for worship and business. Worship meetings consisted of coming together in silence and waiting on the presence of God within each person. There were no set rituals or clergy led services. If an individual felt moved to speak, they did so.

Business meetings attended to the administrative and organizational affairs of the community. These were typically separate from worship meetings and involved discussions and decision-making regarding matters such as finances, property management, membership and community concerns. Overall, Quaker meetings served as vital centers of spiritual worship and community engagement. They provided opportunities for Quakers to come together in worshipful silence, to conduct the business of the community, and to nurture their shared faith and values.

The Indulged Meeting was the lowest in the church organization. This Meeting was organized by the Monthly Meeting at the request of Friends in a new community. It was for worship only. The next was the Preparative Meeting. This Meeting conducted its own business relative to local affairs and kept records. Above that was the Monthly Meeting, which was often composed of a number of Indulged and Preparative Meetings. To and through this Meeting, all business affecting the community came. It could receive and disown members. Above the Monthly Meeting was the Quarterly Meeting. This meeting received cases of appeal, set up new Monthly Meetings and attended to the business of the church on a larger scale, as reports came to it from the several Monthly Meetings under its direction. Annually, Friends came from all parts of a given section of country to consider and act upon matters which concerned the work of the whole church in their particular section, and these were termed Yearly Meetings. The Yearly Meeting held final jurisdiction among its members in all cases regarding church organization.

GEORGE MEACHAM HOLADAY

George was about 5'8 inches tall with fair complexion, blue eyes and light brown hair. He was the son of North Carolina Quakers Samuel and Dolly (Meacham) Holaday. George's paternal great grandfather, Quaker Henry Holaday, Sr., was a Revolutionary War patriot whose family line came from Ireland circa 1713. This author's mother became a member of the Daughters of the American Revolution through this line.

Quakers, being pacifists, were staunchly against the bearing of arms. Their participation in the Revolutionary War was largely in non-combat roles, if at all. Most remained neutral, but a fair number of Quakers did participate. They dealt with repercussions, such as disownment, as a result. Henry's role was that he "provided material aid," in providing a horse for the Americans.

The Holaday name is often spelled or misspelled as "Holiday," "Holliday," and even "Holladay." For purposes of uniformity, the "Holaday" spelling will be used in this book.

The Quakers of the Carolinas were facing increasing persecution due to their disapproval of slavery. They were among the first to denounce slavery and played a major role in the abolitionist movement. They were the first organization to take a collective stand against both slavery and the slave trade. North Carolina state laws, however, prohibited Quakers from legally freeing their slaves without paying exorbitant fees. From 1772 forward, the North Carolina Yearly Meeting advised members that they were not allowed to be involved in the buying and selling of slaves, but they did allow it exclusively between Quakers. The reasoning was that Quaker owners would ensure kind treatment and not split up families. Quakers fed, clothed, housed and treated their slaves with kindness and care, unlike far too many slave owners of the time. In 1781, the North Carolina Yearly Meeting made slavery a disownable offense.

Quakers were fleeing slave states heading to points west. In 1811, Johnathon Lindley, a Quaker abolitionist, land speculator and former legislator, led a group of about thirty North Carolina Quakers and freed former slaves from central North Carolina to Indiana. Even freed slaves had compelling reasons to leave North Carolina, as the "black codes" stripped them of rights. They also faced the constant threat of being kidnapped and sold back into slavery. Some of those in the group were former slaves whose freedom had been purchased by the Quakers, while others were free citizens seeking to flee racial persecution in the South. Traveling with the Quakers afforded them a degree of protection, as well as the promise of good neighbors once they arrived at their destination. They banded together, often with their Quaker neighbors, to survive raids, kidnappings and hostilities from white settlers.

In Indiana, Lindley founded a settlement near Lick Creek, which become known as the Lick Creek Settlement. This was near modern day Paoli, Indiana in Orange County, about fifty miles northwest of Louisville, Kentucky. The settlement welcomed freed former slaves and provided refuge to escaping enslaved people.

Samuel's father, William, (George's grandfather), and some family members may have been with Lindley's group. A "William Holaday," presumably George's grandfather, was granted land on December 24, 1812 in Orange Township (changed to Paoli in 1817). Samuel's uncle, Robert Holaday, with wife Edith (Davis) Holaday, likely made the journey with William. On March 17, 1812, Robert was also granted land in Paoli.

Samuel and Dolly married on March 28, 1814, in Orange County, North Carolina, and left to go to Lick Creek/Paoli soon after. Samuel's second great uncle, Robert Holaday, along with his wife Hannah, two sons and five daughters, arrived in October of 1815, possibly traveling with Samuel and Dolly. Samuel appears on a list of voters in Paoli in November 1816.

When Indiana became a state in 1816, the constitution of the state prohibited slavery, but it did not grant blacks the right to vote, testify in court against whites, join the militia or educate their children in public schools. What they could do, however, was buy land – and they did. At its height in the 1850s, black land ownership in Lick Creek peaked at about 2,300 acres.

In 1813, the Quakers built a meeting house at Lick Creek and established the Lick Creek Monthly Meeting. Some researchers believe Lick Creek was involved in the Underground Railroad and

Background

have found evidence to indicate so. By the nature of the Underground Railroad, however – secrecy – records and information are hard to obtain and verify. A log home built by a Lindley descendant was found to have a small spit with a secret trap door in front of the chimney, believed to be used to hide slaves.

Samuel and Dolly's first child, William, was born on December 14, 1816 in Paoli, Indiana. George was the next born child of seven total children, also born in Paoli, on October 8, 1818.

At the height of Lick Creek's population in the mid-1800s, the settlement had about 200 families. It is unknown exactly why, but an exodus from the area of the black families began about 1862. Some of the remaining population bought the land and continued farming until the Great Depression hit, and they couldn't pay their taxes. The federal government then bought many tax-delinquent and abandoned farms, creating the Hoosier National Forest. There is almost nothing left of the settlement, save some headstones in the Thomas and Roberts Family Cemetery, also known as the Little Africa Cemetery, deep in the heart of the Hoosier National Forest.

When George was ten years old in 1828, Samuel, Dolly and family moved west again. They were "received on certificate" from the Lick Creek Monthly Meeting to the Vermilion (Illinois) Monthly Meeting on March 1, 1828. George's father Samuel was appointed an "overseer" on July 5, 1828. This was a person appointed to look after the wellbeing of those in a Quaker Meeting. Such people were said to be particularly skilled in sensing the needs of others and in knowing how to respond. Samuel died sometime after his July 5, 1828 appointment and before 1837. I suspect he likely died about 1829. Dolly became active in the church, but Samuel is not listed after 1828.

Dolly in the Vermilion Monthly Meeting records:

October 2, 1830: Dolly appointed to visit MacKanaw and Elwood Meeting.

May 7, 1831: Dolly to attend Quarterly Meeting

August 1, 1835: Dolly appointed overseer Hopewell

August 6, 1835: Dolly appointed overseer

George's father Samuel was one of thirteen children born to William and Jane (Andrew) Holaday. Four of Samuel's siblings died before they were ten years old.

George's mother Dolly was one of six children born to Quakers George and Mary (Durham) Meacham, hence the "Meacham" middle name of both George Meacham Holaday and his first-born son Samuel. Both George and Mary's fathers were Revolutionary War patriots, as was her brother, Matthew Durham, Jr. (1760-1834). Dolly's parents are buried in the "Meacham Graves" in Paoli, Orange County, Indiana. The Lost River Chapter of the Daughters of the American Revolution documented the following concerning the graves of Dolly's parents:

"Meacham Graves - From the Cemetery Records compiled by the Lost River Chapter DAR, Paoli Township Sec. 34-T. 2N.-R.1W. Obliterated. In a field, just west of Newberry Cemetery, are the graves of George Meacham and his wife, early settlers from North Carolina. The family lived about three miles north of Newberry, and at the time of George Meacham's death, there was a plan to open a public burying ground at this place. Only the two Meachams were buried here and it is probable that the plan was abandoned with the opening of the Friend's cemetery, a few years later. For many years the little burial plot was kept fenced by descendants, but has now been plowed over. Isaac Meacham, a son, and Ruth McVey, a daughter, are buried in the old Paoli Cemetery. The graves had markers of field stones, no inscriptions."

LYDIA HOLLINGSWORTH HOLADAY

Figure 1: Lydia Hollingsworth Holaday. Photo courtesy of Jill Foster Livingston, third great granddaughter of George & Lydia Holaday.

George's wife Lydia was born in Union County, Indiana to Quakers Ezekiel Hollingsworth and Jane Hollingsworth. Lydia was the sixth great granddaughter of Quaker Valentine Hollingsworth Sr., the progenitor of most of the American Hollingsworths. (daughter of Ezekial, of Joseph, of George, of Abraham, of Thomas, of Valentine Sr.) Valentine came to the New World from Ireland on the ship *Antelope* with his family in 1682 and was part of William Penn's colony of Quakers in Delaware. Valentine had been converted to Quakerism in Ireland. William Penn granted Valentine 968 acres of land in modern day Wilmington, Delaware. Valentine was one of the signers of William Penn's Great Charter, which established the principles of government of Pennsylvania. William Penn founded the city of Philadelphia, Pennsylvania.

Ezekiel and Jane were from South Carolina, marrying there about 1802. Ezekiel was the son of Joseph Hollingsworth of Virginia and Margaret Wright of Maryland. Jane was the daughter of George Hollingsworth of Virginia (1762-1824) and Jane Henry of South Carolina (1759 -?). Ezekiel and Jane's fathers were step-brothers - making Ezekiel and Jane first half-cousins.

Ezekiel's family had emigrated to South Carolina circa 1765, near the area of Newberry, and many joined the Bush River Quaker Monthly Meeting there. Quakers were attracted to South Carolina because of the colony's religious freedom and tolerance, as well as its economic opportunity. The colony did not require that settlers practice a specific faith.

Many South Carolina Quakers, as their northern counterparts, grew increasingly disturbed by the immorality and cruelty of the slavery system. They recognized that the violence required for the maintenance of the institution of slavery contradicted their pacifist beliefs. As part of the North Carolina Yearly Meeting, the Bush River Monthly Meeting followed their instructions on the buying, selling and hiring of slaves.

The dependence on slave labor was a foundational part of South Carolina's development and culture. It had the most rigid "slave codes" so as to ensure the success of its slave society. South Carolinian masters were granted total control over their slaves. The Negro Act of 1740 prohibited slaves from learning to read and write. Like North Carolina, South Carolina also prohibited the freeing of slaves. South Carolina had larger slave populations than North Carolina and had greater economic dependence on slavery.

Many of the Bush River Quakers worked through the North Carolina Yearly Meeting to help slaves escape their bondage. One method was to take them to the North Carolina Quakers, where they were provided with good places to live and work with some semblance of freedom. From there, they could be transported to free territory or to colonies in Western Africa or Haiti.

The 1800s brought with it an expansion of slavery in South Carolina, due to the growth of cotton crops. This led to a massive exodus of Quakers from Bush River and other southern states as well – numbering in the tens of thousands. This exodus became known as the "Great Migration" in Quaker literature. Many Bush River Quakers sold their farms, abandoned their slaves or sold them to the North Carolina Yearly Meeting. They loaded all their essential items on wagons and headed to Ohio or beyond.

Lydia's father Ezekiel found himself in trouble with the Quakers from time to time. On June 26, 1802, he was found guilty of "fighting and drinking strong liquor to excess, frequenting taverns and trespassing against his neighbor in throwing down the fence." He made his amends and on September 25, 1802 it was noted that he "produced an offering to this meeting which this meeting is free to receive as satisfaction."

The following year, on May 25, 1803 he was back in trouble, this time found guilty of "drinking strong drink to excess and fighting."

Apparently, Ezekiel did not apologize and was disowned in October of 1803 from the Bush River Monthly Meeting. It is not known if he made amends to be readmitted at Bush River. When disowned, Quakers could still attend Meeting for worship and interact with family and friends, but they were no longer "under the care of Meeting." They could no longer attend business meetings or hold a position. Disownment was not punishment, but rather, their way of ensuring that those under the care of the Meeting followed rules that contributed to the community's best interests. In most cases, a written apology acknowledging and condemning their actions, along with changed behavior, was all that was necessary for reinstatement in the Meeting after disownment.

In 1803, an itinerant Quaker preacher, Zachary Dix, visited Bush River. His words would be a catalyst for the Bush River Quakers. He addressed the community, proclaiming:

"O Bush River, Bush River, how hath thy beauty faded away and gloomy darkness eclipsed thy day! My Master, whom I serve continually, hath sent me here with a little message of warning. For almost one half a century God has prospered you… Have not the recent winds from the south borne to us the awful curse in the massacre of San Domingo, telling the tragic story of human slavery?[1] God made of one blood all the races of the Earth... But O Bush River, there are those of the number who have forsaken the God of their fathers! You are depriving your fellow men of the God given rights. You have bought them like cattle in the pen; you have sold them like sheep at the slaughter. You have counted them among your assets; you have listed them as your property, the same as your cotton and your corn. There are those within the sound of my voice, to whom conscience has been saying, lo these many years, in the language of the prophet of old, 'Under the heavy burdens, break free every chain and let the oppressed go free.'"

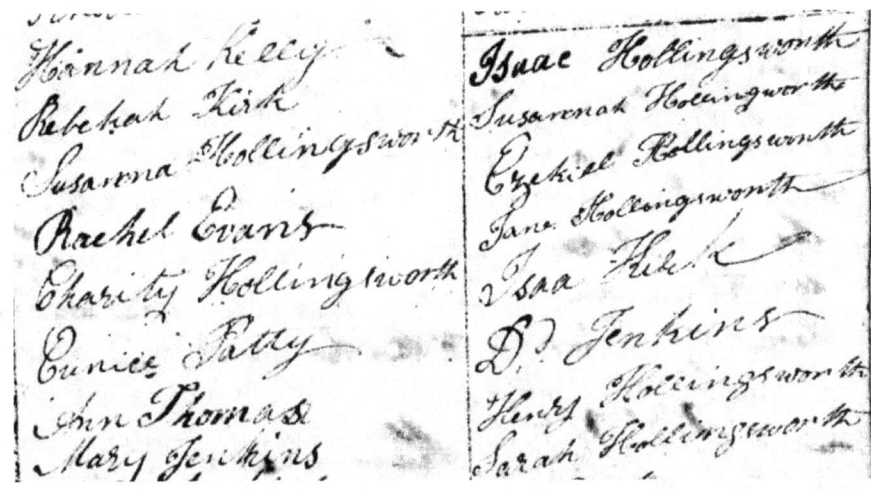

Figure 2: Bush River Monthly Meeting record of some of the witnesses who attended the Hollingsworth/Stanton marriage on May 2, 1805, with many of the Hollingsworths in attendance.

On May 2, 1805, Ezekiel, wife Jane and a number of Hollingsworths attended the Quaker wedding of Sarah

---

[1] On August 22, 1791, the slaves of San Domingo / Saint Domingue rose up in rebellion, initiating what was to become, over the next several years, the first successful slave revolt in history. San Domingo became Haiti in 1804.

Hollingsworth and Samuel Stanton in Bush River. Sarah was Ezekiel's first cousin. Also in 1805, Ezekiel and Jane's first child, a son named Zebulon, was born.

There was a mass Quaker exodus from South Carolina between the years of 1802 and 1807, with the majority of its members gone by 1808. Circa 1805, the migration of the South Carolina Hollingsworths began. Many of them headed to Miami County, Ohio to join the Miami Monthly Meeting.

After Ezekiel and family left South Carolina, they are next found in Dearborn County, Indiana Territory, in 1809. A daughter, Mary, was born in 1808, likely in Indiana. Dearborn County was organized in 1803 by Governor William Henry Harrison, who named it after General Henry Dearborn, at that time the Secretary of War under President Thomas Jefferson. It is about 35 miles west and slightly north of Cincinnati, Ohio. As boundary lines changed, it would eventually be downsized, with Franklin and Union Counties assuming some of its original area.

On April 3, 1809, Ezekiel was at an election held at the home of John Templeton, Esquire, in what is now Quakertown in Union County, Indiana. They were voting for territorial representation in the sixth election district of the county of Dearborn. Ten Hollingsworth men voted.

John Templeton had come to Indiana about 1801 with a group from Laurens County, South Carolina, and established the "Carolina Colony," located on the East Fork of the Whitewater River. John's cabin was built in 1805 and was two stories tall with a fireplace located on both floors. He was appointed the first justice of the peace in 1806, serving the northern part of Dearborn County. It is likely that Ezekiel and family lived near or in the "Carolina Colony" settlement. Many years later the cabin was relocated and today sits on the Union County Courthouse square in Liberty, Indiana.

Background

On July 22, 1809, in Dearborn County, Ezekiel signed as a witness to a land sale. On December 12, 1809, Ezekiel's name is on a petition to Congress by male citizens of Indiana Territory. The signors protested being deprived of the right of suffrage, saying they believed it to be the birthright of every American. More specifically, the right of every free, white male who paid taxes and/or performed militia duty.

The entire petition reads as follows. It is printed exactly as it appears in the digitized version of the Territorial Papers, with no spelling or punctuation corrections. (Carter, 1939)

PETITION TO CONGRESS BY CITIZENS OF THE TERRITORY

(HF : 11 Cong ., 2 sess .: DS] [Referred December 12, 1809]

To the Honorable the Senate and house of Representatives of the united States in Congress Assembled--

The petition of the subscribers citizens of the Indiana Territory humbly prays and Sheweth, that by the Ordinance for the Government of the Territory, a great number of the Citizens are deprived of the right of Suffrage, a right which we conceive to be the birthright of every American, and which we suppose to be guarrenteed to us by that Constitution which declares that all men by Nature are born equaly free-- That we are compelled to contribute to our county and Territorial taxes and withall do militia duty and are at the same time Deprived of haveing even an indirect voice in the Appointment of the men who are entrusted with the disposal of that money which is gathered almost entirely from the earnings of the farming intrest-- In short we are deprived of nearly all the rights of American Citizens, but are compelled to perform all the duties thereof-- We therefore fondly hope that we shall not ask what ought not to be granted; when we pray that the Right of Suffrage may be extended, to every free white male inhabitant in said territory who shall have attained the age of twenty one years and who shall have paid a County or Territorial tax – or done militia duty, --and that the people may be enabled to choose their own Officers both Civil and Militia-- and your petitioners as in duty bound will ever pray &c...

The petition was signed by 161 men, nine of which were Hollingsworths. Most of the signers of the petition to Congress also voted in the election.

Ezekiel and Jane most likely had most of the rest of their children in Union County, Indiana: Jeremiah, Mahundry, Miles, Cynthia, John, William, Lydia, Elias and Eliza. Elias and Eliza were twins. Their last child, Ruth Jane, was born in Vermilion County, Illinois. There is some evidence that daughter Cynthia may have been born in Cynthiana, Indiana, although no records have been found as of yet to confirm such.

It is not known when Ezekiel and family were readmitted to the Quakers, but certainly by 1815, when they were "received by request" at the Whitewater Monthly Meeting in Wayne County, Indiana.

Quaker records indicate that the family next relocated to Kokomo in Howard County, Indiana. This is further substantiated by a passage in Lydia's obituary stating that she spent her early girlhood in Kokomo. About 1824, the family relocated near Danville in Vermilion County, Illinois, just over the Indiana border. (Vermilion County, Illinois and Vermillion County, Indiana border one another.)

It would seem that shortly after arrival in Vermilion County, Illinois, Lydia's mother Jane passed away. Lydia would have been about six years old. Extensive searching of Quaker records has yet to reveal a death record. The earliest she could have died would have been August 25, 1825, as that is the date of their last child, Ruth's, birth. Ezekiel was active in Vermilion County, Illinois, but there is no mention of Jane. It has become my suspicion that Jane may have died in childbirth or shortly thereafter.

Ezekiel in the Vermilion Monthly Meeting records:

June 7, 1828: Ezekiel and Jacob on committee to receive accounts of suffering cases on account of military demands.

April 4, 1829: Ezekiel to attend Quarterly Meeting.

August 9, 1830: Ezekiel on committee to secure teacher for Vermilion school.

June 2, 1832: Ezekiel on committee to revise and record minutes.

June 6, 1835: Ezekiel to assist recording names of families.

December 5, 1835: Ezekiel appointed overseer.

February 4, 1837: Ezekiel on education committee.

April 7, 1837: Ezekiel on education committee.

The first school in Vermilion County, Illinois was a log school house in Elwood Township. Reuben Black opened the school in the winter of 1824-1825 and taught one winter. There were fourteen pupils, among which were Ezekiel's sons Jeremiah, Miles, Mahundry and John.

On May 10, 1837, Ezekiel married again. Interestingly enough, he married George M. Holaday's mother Dolly. They were wed in a Quaker ceremony at the Hopewell Meeting house in Vermillion County, Indiana.

Both George and Lydia were present as witnesses, as was Ezekiel's son Zebulon, and Dolly's daughter Sarah.

Background

George M. Holaday
b: 08 Oct 1818 Orange Co., Indiana, USA
d: 05 Sep 1895 Tulare, California, USA

- **Samuel Holaday**
  b: 02 Feb 1790 Orange Co., North Carolina, USA
  d: Bet. 1828-1836 USA
  - **William Holaday**
    b: 10 Aug 1750 New Garden, Chester, Pennsylvania, USA
    d: Abt. 1815 Paoli, Orange, Indiana, USA
    - **Henry Holaday Sr**
      b: 1725 Chester Co., PA, USA
      d: 09 Sep 1800 Chatham County, North Carolina, USA
    - **Mary Fayle**
      b: 1725 Wilmington, New Castle, Delaware, USA
      d: 21 Jun 1797 Chatham County, North Carolina, USA
  - **Jane Andrew**
    b: 12 Nov 1755 Chester, Pennsylvania, USA
    d: Orange County, Indiana, USA
    - **Robert Andrew**
      b: 1725 Cane Creek, Orange, North Carolina, USA
      d: 12 Jan 1791 Cane Creek, Orange, North Carolina, USA
    - **Sarah Anders**
      b: 1728 Cane Creek, Orange, North Carolina, USA
      d: 1777 Cane Creek, Orange, North Carolina, USA
- **Dolly Meacham**
  b: 24 Oct 1793 Chatham, North Carolina, USA
  d: Aft. 1845
  - **George Meacham**
    b: 1765 Virginia, USA
    d: 1819 Paoli, Orange, Indiana, USA
    - **William S. Meacham**
      b: 1725 Middlesex County, Virginia, USA
      d: Aug 1808 Chatham, North Carolina, USA
    - **Elizabeth Crutchfield**
      b: 1740 Middlesex County, Virginia, USA
      d: 1813 Chatham, North Carolina, USA
  - **Mary Durham**
    b: 01 Jan 1769 Orange County, North Carolina, USA
    d: 1823 Paoli, Orange, Indiana, USA
    - **Matthew Durham Sr**
      b: 29 Jul 1731 Orange Co., North Carolina, USA
      d: 09 Dec 1795 Orange Co., North Carolina, USA
    - **Susannah Lindsey**
      b: 20 Jul 1731 Brunswick, Virginia, USA
      d: 30 May 1799 Orange Co., North Carolina, USA

George's Parents

SAMUEL HOLADAY (of William, of Henry Sr., of Robert, of William James) born: 02 Feb 1790, Orange Co., NC; died: between 1828-1836; mar: DOLLY MEACHAM, daughter of George Meacham and Mary Durham, 28 Mar 1814, Orange County, NC; born: 24 Oct 1793, Chatham, NC; died: after 1845

George's Siblings

WILLIAM HOLADAY, born: 14 Dec 1816, Orange County, IN; died: 1879, Vermilion County, IL; mar: ELIZABETH JANE HAWORTH, 04 Apr 1839, Vermilion County, IL; born: 26 Jun 1819, TN; died: 18 Aug 1899, Vermillion, IL. Children: Mary Ann, James Perry, Anna Mariah, George Murray, Angeline, Thomas, Cassius M., Inez

JANE HOLADAY, born: 20 Jan 1821, Orange County, IN; died: 1880, Manning, IA; mar 1: JOHN HOLLINGSWORTH, son of Ezekiel Hollingsworth and Jane Hollingsworth, 16 Nov 1837, Vermillion, IN; born: 1816, IN; died: 18 Aug 1854, Keokuk County, IA. Children: Elias, Frances Jane, George Edwin. mar 2: WILLIAM TINGLE DR, son of John Edward Tingle and Clarissa Bishop, 27 May 1845, Keokuk, IA; born: 06 Apr 1810, VA; died: 28 Nov 1886, Bassett, NE. Children: John M., Albert Holaday, William Oscar, Mary Ellen, Darcy S., Samuel C., Effie D.

SARAH HOLADAY, born: 13 Dec 1822 Orange County, IN; died: possibly 1866 Council Bluffs, IA (unsubstantiated)

ASENATH HOLADAY, born: 08 Dec 1824, Orange County, IN; died: 18 Dec 1864, Council Bluffs, IA; mar: FRANKLIN STREET, son of Aaron Mannington Street and Cecilia Dunavan, 18 Aug 1842, Washington, Iowa; born: 07 Dec 1819 Blunt, TN; died: 17 Feb 1877, Council Bluffs, IA. Children: Cyrus Holaday, Sheridan Dunivan, Eugene Aaron, Chastine A., Hortense Dolly, Willis Franklin, Edgar Fremont, May Cecelia

ELIZABETH "BETSEY" ANN HOLADAY, born: 22 Dec 1826, Orange County, IN; died: 16 Nov 1861, Union Co., IN; mar: SETH KELLY, son of Willis Kelly and Charity Hollingsworth, 04 Apr 1844, Union, IN; born: 01 Dec 1818, Liberty, IN; died: 03 Apr 1886, Liberty, IN. Children: Donna Martha, Alpha R., Jane Olive, Capron C., Lina Bell, Addie Estella, Minnie B.

RUTH ANN HOLADAY, born: Feb 1829, IL; died: 15 Mar 1903, Bradford, PA; mar JOHN MILTON WILLIS, born: about 1829, England; died: 1884. Children: George, Alice M., Edward Darwin, Walter John, Frank Herbert, Mary Elizabeth.

Background

Lydia Hollingsworth
b: 23 Nov 1819 Union, Indiana, USA
d: 08 Jul 1911 Winterset, Madison, Iowa, USA

Ezekiel Hollingsworth
b: 1781 South Carolina, USA
d: Abt. 1843 Richland, Keokuk, Iowa, USA

Joseph Hollingsworth
b: 1735 Frederick County, Virginia, USA
d: 10 Sep 1792 Bush River, Newberry, South Carolina, USA

George H. Hollingsworth
b: 07 Apr 1712 Newark, Cecil, Maryland, USA
d: 16 Nov 1786 Laurens, Newberry County, South Carolina, USA

Hannah McCoy
b: 1717 Augusta, Frederick, Virginia, USA
d: 1754 Augusta, Frederick, Virginia, USA

Margaret Wright
b: 12 Jan 1742 Queen Anne, Prince George, Maryland, USA
d: 13 Nov 1822 Laurens County, South Carolina, USA

John C. Wright
b: 04 Nov 1716 East Nottingham, Chester, Pennsylvania, USA
d: 08 Jun 1790 Bush River, Newberry, South Carolina, USA

Rachel Wells
b: 27 Mar 1720 All Hallows Parish, Anne Arundel Co., Maryland, USA
d: 23 Dec 1771 Bush River, Newberry, South Carolina, USA

Jane Hollingsworth
b: 1783 Saluda, South Carolina, USA
d: Bet. 1825-1836 Indiana

George Hollingsworth
b: 1762 Frederick, Virginia, USA
d: 12 Apr 1824 Darke, Ohio, USA

George H. Hollingsworth
b: 07 Apr 1712 Newark, Cecil, Maryland, USA
d: 16 Nov 1786 Laurens, Newberry County, South Carolina, USA

Jane E. Carter
b: 1720 Frederick, Virginia, USA
d: 07 Jun 1795 Bush River, Newberry County, South Carolina, USA

Jane Henry
b: 1759 South Carolina, South Carolina, USA

Name:

Name:

See Lydia's parent and sibling information on page 146.

CHAPTER 2
CONTRARY TO DISCIPLINE

Eighteen months after their parents' marriage, on November 29, 1838, George and Lydia married in a civil ceremony in Vermilion County, Illinois. Lydia was nineteen years old, and George was twenty. Their parents had married one another and now they had married as well.

Quakers were required to marry only other Quakers, as well as to marry according to the church's procedures. Not doing so usually led to disownment. Ezekiel and Dolly were active members in high standing, so one must wonder if they were disappointed or upset about their children's civil marriage. Depending on the strictness of the Meeting, they may not have been able to even attend their children's civil wedding without risk of their own disownment.

Procedure for a Quaker marriage differed remarkably from traditional marriage. There was a process that could take weeks or even months before the marriage would be blessed by the church.

Many did not care to go through the process and married in a civil ceremony, as George and Lydia did. In order to follow the rule of the church, first the man and woman concerned were required to inform the overseers of the Preparative Meeting to which the woman belonged of the proposed union. The two parties next appeared at the succeeding Monthly Meeting, with evidence in hand that they had informed both the men's and the women's Meeting of their intentions. At that point, each body appointed a committee of two of its members.

The men were to investigate the man's "clearness of like engagements with others," while the women were to do the same for the bride-to-be. Once accomplished, at the following Monthly Meeting, the committees gave their reports. If satisfactory, the parties concerned were then to go together into both the men's and women's meetings and publicly declare their "continued intentions of marriage." When each and all of these acts had been recorded in the minutes, the parties would propose a date for their wedding. Finally, each of the Meetings appointed another committee of two of its members to be present and see that "good order be observed."

George and Lydia's choice not to go through the lengthy Quaker procedures led to them both being disowned. George found himself in trouble with the Quakers even before the marriage, however. Apparently, in the prior winter, he had "attended a place of diversion at the time called Christmas." Such a place or event could have been a stage-play, horse race, music show, a dance or one of many other miscellaneous sports or amusements. The problem likely wasn't that it was during Christmas, as Quakers of that time did not celebrate Christmas, but it was because of the place he went or event he attended.

On April 6, 1839, the Vermilion Monthly Meeting reported that, "Hopewell Preparative Meeting informs that George M. Holaday has accomplished his marriage contrary to discipline, and associated with a company in exercising in vain sport at the time called Christmas. Richard Haworth and Samuel Stanfield are appointed to visit him on the occasion, and report their sense of the disposition of his mind to next meeting."

At the next meeting on May 4, 1839, it was reported, "The Friends appointed to visit George M. Holaday again report they have extended thereto and still believe him not in a disposition to make satisfaction which being considered the meeting unites in disowning him and appoints (illegible) Henderson and Jonathon Haworth to prepare a testimony against him and inform him thereof and produce it to next meeting."

The final step was to prepare the testimony, which was done and reported at the next Meeting on June 1, 1839: "The Friends appointed to prepare a testimony of denial against George M. Holaday produced the following: George M. Holaday who has had a right of membership in the Society of Friends, has accomplished his marriage contrary to discipline and associated with a company in vain diversions at the time called Christmas for which he has been treated without the desired affect; we therefore disown him from being a member with us." A Friend was appointed to offer George a copy of the order and inform him of his right to appeal. He did not appeal. On July 7, 1839, the report of May 4 was approved and George was officially disowned.

Oddly, I have not been able to document Lydia's disownment in the Quaker records but it is certain that she was disowned as well. The term marrying "contrary to discipline" was used when two Quakers married outside the procedures of the Church, so this indicates Lydia was indeed a Quaker prior to their marriage. Another term that is often seen is marrying "out of unity." The latter means a Quaker married a non-Quaker. Due to the use of "contrary to discipline," we can assume she was a member in good standing prior to the marriage.

This would prove to be a devastating loss for Lydia. An excerpt of her obituary states, "Born in the Friends' faith, she was the greater part of her life unable to attend a church of her belief, yet she lived always according to its truest creedal spirit, being a deep and untiring reader of the Bible, and a searcher for its hidden and inspired meanings."

Their first child, Samuel Meacham Holaday, was born in Vermillion County, Indiana on November 8, 1839. He would be the only child born there. Ten more children would be born over the next twenty-one years: John Milton, Miles, Caroline, Ellen, Emma, William, Thomas Jefferson, Orpha, Pauline and Henry Delano. Ellen and Emma were twins. Thomas Jefferson and Orpha both died young.

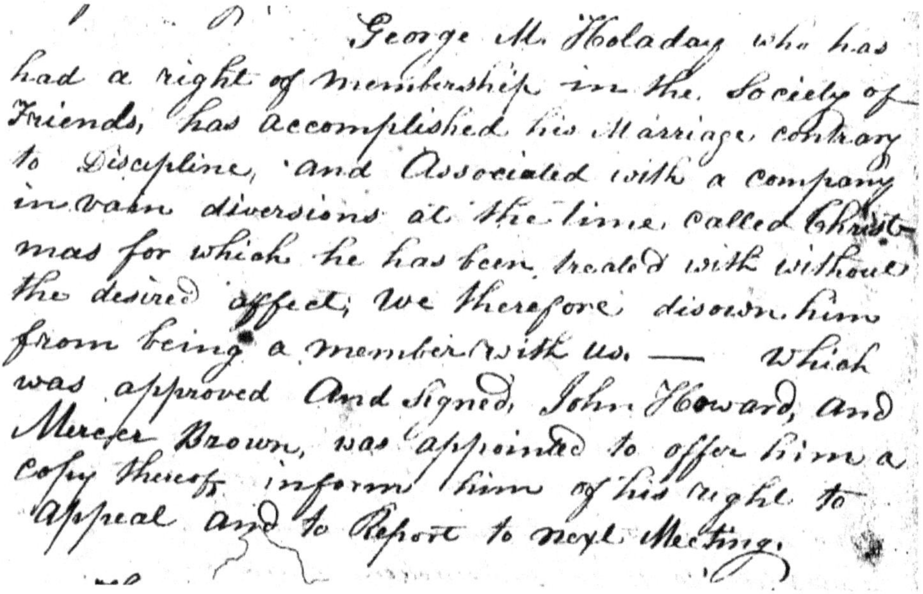

Figure 3: Vermilion, Illinois Monthly Meeting record of George's disownment

CHAPTER 3
THE "NEW LANDS"- IOWA TERRITORY

I had never rode through a country so full of game.

Indian Agent, Joseph Street, 1833

The United States Congress established the territory of Iowa on July 4, 1838. At that time, it included much of today's Minnesota and half of the Dakotas, but only went as far west as modern-day Des Moines. In 1840, the population of Iowa Territory was about 43,000 and there were only eighteen established counties.

Early settlers found Iowa to be very different from the eastern United States. In the east, the land was covered almost entirely with forests and wood was plentiful. In eastern Iowa, they still found enough wood for homes, barns, fences and fuel, but in some areas, there was only enough wood to construct buildings.

Iowa was once 70-80% covered with tallgrass prairies, an ocean of treeless grasslands, some up to twelve feet tall. It resembled water when the breeze blew, undulating like waves. In these areas, pioneers had to burn prairie hay and corn cobs for fuel.

In 1840 Dr. Isaac Galland noted a large number of fauna in Iowa, including bison, elk, deer (either white-tailed deer or mule deer), raccoon, fox squirrel, mountain lion, lynx, gray wolf, black wolf, coyote (he called them prairie wolves), bear, beaver, otter, muskrat, mink, rabbits (presumably cottontail rabbit and hare), opossum, skunk, porcupine, groundhog, timber rattlesnake, prairie rattlesnake, bull snake, black snake, water moccasin, garter snake, water snakes, turkey, prairie chicken, quail, swan, geese, brant goose, duck, crane (he called them pelicans), crow, blackbird, bald eagle, "grey eagle" (probably a hawk or falcon), buzzard, raven, mourning dove, passenger pigeon, woodpeckers, woodcocks, hummingbird, and the honeybee.[2]

In 1840, George, Lydia, son Samuel, all of Lydia's siblings and their spouses, her father Ezekiel, George's mother Dolly and four of George's siblings headed west to Iowa Territory.

Prior to leaving, Ezekiel and his son Jeremiah sold off most, if not all, of their land holdings in Vermilion County, Illinois, presumably to fund their journey and new lives in Iowa. Ezekiel made a land sale for $800, equivalent today to about $29,000. One of Jeremiah's land sales was for $420, equivalent to about $15,000. No doubt others sold their holdings as well.

Before setting out, they would have spent considerable time studying maps and seeking advice from travelers familiar with the area. Their route would have been one that minimized obstacles and maximized access to water and natural resources.

---

[2] Dr. Isaac Galland was a merchant, postmaster, land speculator and doctor. He lived in unorganized territory of Iowa in 1829 – four years before permanent settlement began in Iowa. He founded the first school in what would become Iowa Territory.

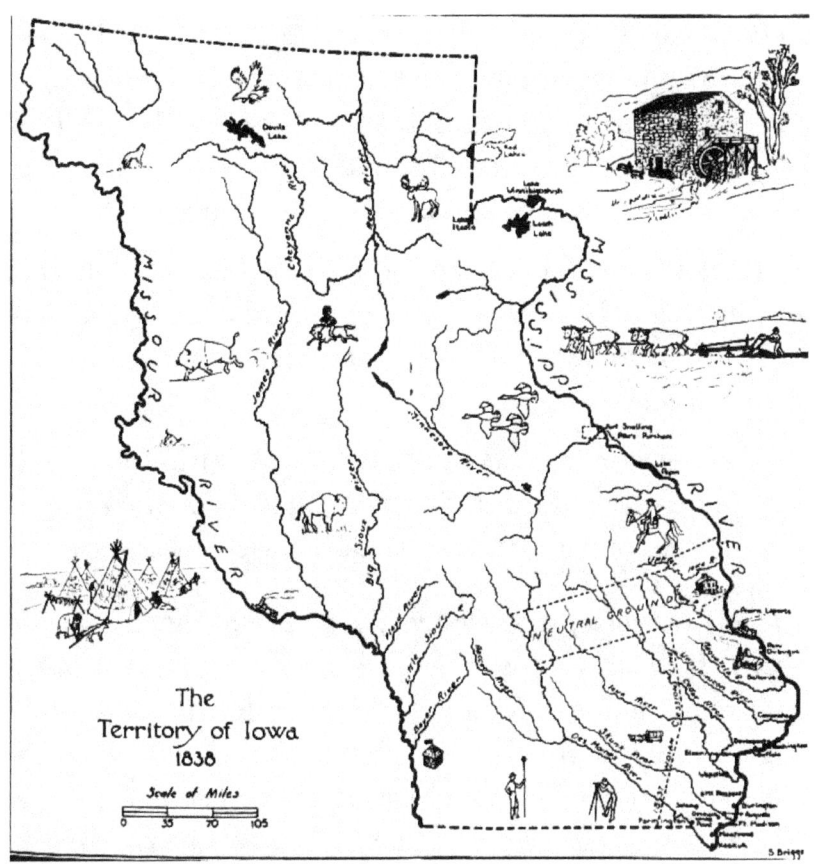

Figure 4: S. Briggs, The Territory of Iowa, 1838. *The Palimpsest 44 (6), State Historical Society of Iowa, 1963*

Preparing for the trip would have required gathering necessary supplies and provisions for the journey. This would include food, water, tools, spare parts for wagons, clothing, and other essentials.

They loaded up all they owned in wagons, pulled by oxen. Their destination was about 350 miles away, through all manner of topography; forest, prairie, farmland, woodlands and rolling hills.

There were few roads and no bridges. Water crossings were time consuming and often dangerous. For the larger crossings, such as the Illinois, the Mississippi and the Des Moines Rivers, they would have had to cross via ferry ("flat boat") or raft. In the latter, two canoes would be lashed together and rough boards tied across the top. The wagons would have had to be taken apart and loaded on the makeshift raft, along with all of their possessions. The livestock was forced to swim alongside or behind. Once on the other side, the wagons would need to be reassembled and reloaded.

It is not known what route they chose to follow, but most likely, the Hollingsworths and Holadays crossed the mighty Mississippi, the "Father of Waters," at Rock Island, Illinois and used a ferry or flat boat to get them across.

At a typical rate of ten miles per day, the trip would've taken nearly a month. In *Salem, The Pioneer Quaker Community of Iowa*, Louis T. Jones provides us with valuable insight into pioneer travel:

In these days of modern travel, we can hardly appreciate what such trips across the plains in the early days meant. It took courage to pull away from all of the ties of a settled home and face the dangers of an unsettled and uncivilized west, where the wolf and the savage roamed unrestrained over the broad plains. Usually two, or more, families traveled together for mutual consolation and protection. High wheeled, covered wagons of the schooner type were the usual means of conveyance. The slow plodding oxen, rather than the horse, proved to be the friend of the pioneer on these long trips. Many times the old story of the tortoise and the hare was reenacted in those days; for those who started off with prancing horses hitched to their heavy wagons found themselves passed by the more steady, patient oxen, long before the end of the journey.

In preparing for the trip the wagons were loaded with enough corn meal and smoked meat to last during the journey; the necessary cooking utensils were packed in;

sometimes a few pieces of prized furniture were taken; the farm implements that would be used in breaking the prairie sod and sufficient grain for the first sowing completed the load.

At night the whole company would camp together, and the camp fire would be lighted. Iron skillets and kettles would be brought from the wagons, and the evening meal prepared on the glowing coals. The toils of the day were soon forgotten around these cheerful campfires. In fact, there seems to be something about a campfire, with its ruddy glow, its crackling sparks and its ascending smoke, that cheers the heart of a tired traveler.

When bed time came the women and children retired to the covered wagons, and the men rolled up in their comforts and blankets beneath. Usually one or more of the men remained on guard during the night to keep the cattle from straying, and to protect them from the wolves, whose desolate howl could be heard far and near.

At early dawn the camp was astir. The morning meal was soon over and the caravan again moved off to the westward, leaving as the only mark of their last resting place, the smoldering embers of the camp fire. Happy was such a group of people when they could say that they had reached the end of their journey; and happy was the settlement which could receive the new comers. They were taken in with a hospitality that has become proverbial. They were given the "white bread" as long as it lasted, and made welcome until they could locate a claim and build their own log cabin.

In southeastern Iowa Territory in 1840, many small settlements and homesteads dotted the land, still in very early stages of development. Most were located along river valleys, where fertile land was amenable to farming and access to waterways provided transportation and trade routes.

Native American tribes, namely the Sauk and Fox, had established villages and communities along the river valleys. There were still occasional conflicts between the tribes and the white settlers but many interacted for purposes of trade and community.

The first thing the Hollingsworths and Holadays would have done after staking their claims would have been to construct their cabins. Most cabins were simple affairs, constructed from locally sourced materials.

Despite the isolation of frontier settlements, pioneers formed close-knit communities. Neighbors relied on each other for mutual aid and support, coming together for activities such as cabin building, social gatherings and religious services.

George and Lydia were no longer Quakers, but Ezekiel and Dolly were, as well as were many other family members, so Quaker records help in tracing their movement to and in Iowa Territory.

SALEM, HENRY COUNTY, IOWA

Quaker and abolitionist Aaron Street, Jr. came to Iowa in the fall of 1835 to attempt to locate a place where he could make a settlement of Friends. As he prospected along the Skunk River in Henry County, he was impressed with the beauty of the land – the woods "abounding with fruits and wild honey" and the prairie "bright with autumn flowers."

> *Now have mine eyes beheld a country teeming with every good thing. Hither I will come with my flocks and my herds, with my children and my children's children, and our city shall be called Salem, for thus was the city of our fathers, even near unto the seacoast.*
>
> *Aaron Street, Jr.*

He, along with Issac Pidgeon, who had built his cabin, decided to form a Quaker community and laid out a town site, which they named Salem. It did not take long for many eastern Quakers to also make the journey to Henry County. The Monthly Meeting at Salem was officially established on October 8, 1838, the first Monthly Meeting of the Society of Friends west of the Mississippi.[3] In 1839, attendance at the Salem Meeting was about 300 people. When the Hollingsworths and Holadays arrived, Ezekiel, Dolly and other family members were received into membership.

It appears that they initially all settled in or near Salem. Lydia's brother Jeremiah appears on the 1840 United States Federal Census in Henry County. Soon after, many family members, including George and Lydia, settled about thirty-five miles northwest of Salem, in and near Richland, Iowa in what would become Keokuk County. Richland was a tiny pioneer town on the border of the Indian territory.

Salem, Iowa would become one of the most active Underground Railroad communities in Iowa. The friendly Quaker disposition

---

[3] Vermilion was the parent meeting for Salem Monthly Meeting in Salem, Iowa and all membership certificates went there until Salem became a Monthly Meeting.

The "New Lands" – Iowa Territory

Figure 5: The Settled Counties of Iowa Territory *in 1841 with added arrow to indicate Richland's location. Map by Sidney Edwards Morse circa 1840.*

The "New Lands" – Iowa Territory

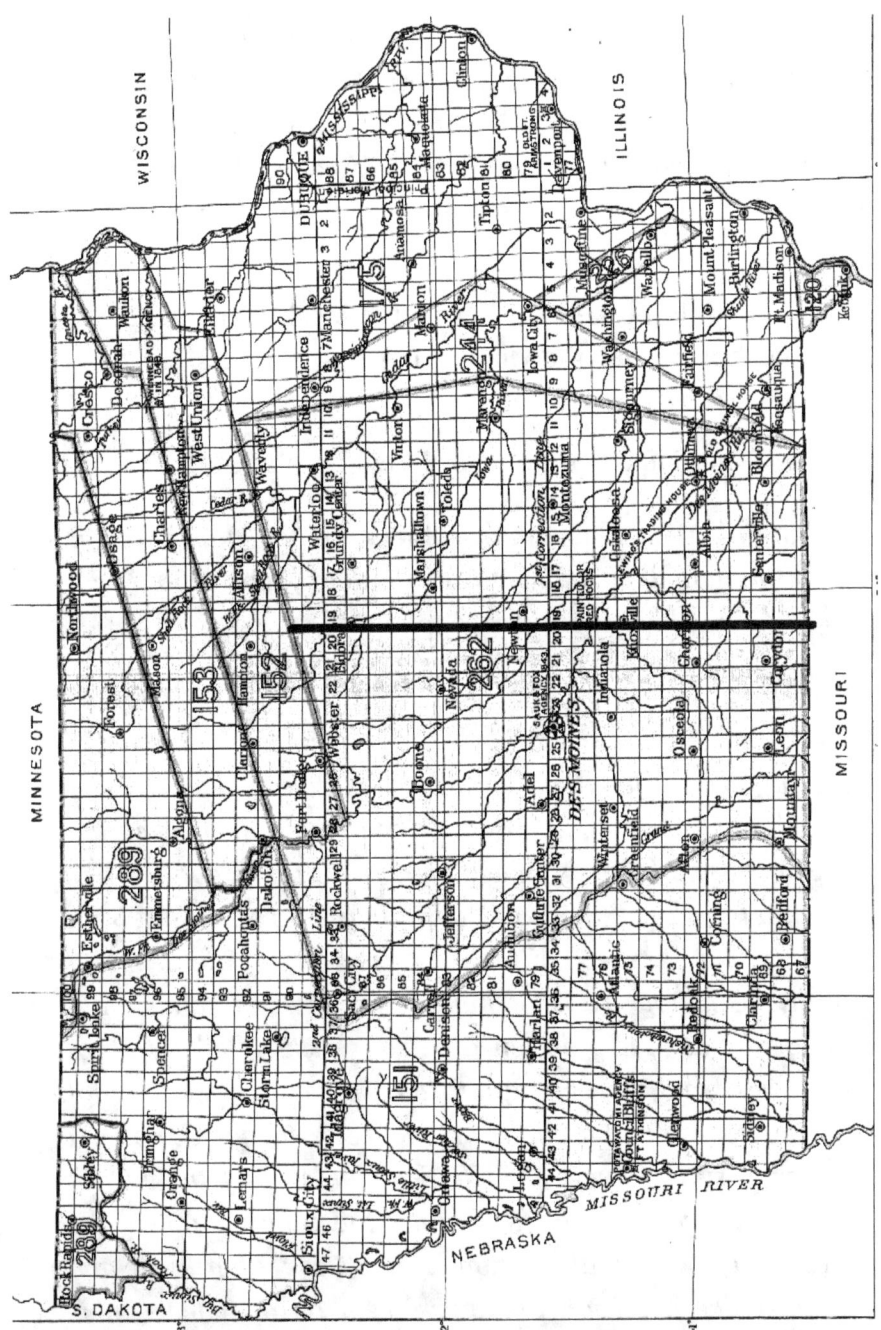

Figure 6: Indian Land Cessions in Iowa. *The thick black line denotes the Red Rock Line. Charles C. Royce and Cyrus Thomas, 1899. Law Library of Congress.*

towards fugitive slaves from Missouri soon became well known. A Salem Quaker, Elihu Frazier, once made a trip to Missouri to tell slaves that they could find welcome in Salem. He was captured by slave patrollers and they attempted to force him to confess that he was offering refuge to slaves, but he refused and was eventually released.

Quaker children were not allowed to speak of anything they saw regarding slaves, and the Quaker meeting minutes contained no records. Secrecy was key.

From *The Quakers of Iowa* by Louis T. Jones, 1914:

Taking his life in his hands, some unknown slave made his way to safety, then another, and another, each opening wider the way for those who were to follow...

... Salem, but twenty-five miles from the Missouri line, and surrounded by numerous wooded streams well adapted for hiding, proved for the Negro a most advantageous place at which to stop for food. The unfailing help which they there received soon became widely known. Could he but reach the town where lived the people of plain grey clothes and broad brimmed hats, the fugitive was assured of safety. ...What with the heavy loads of human freight concealed within hollow loads of hay or beneath grain sacks filled with bran, and the strange proclivity of this Quaker folk for midnight drives to unknown mills or markets, large numbers of fugitive slaves were spirited away to safety by that mysterious route which fitly gained the name: 'Underground Railroad'. Month after month and year after year with Quaker-like precision this work went on at Salem-- not a single slave being retaken, it is said, once he had reached this community. The children in the homes were trained to ask no

questions, much less to answer any asked by strangers. They were supposed to have no eyes or no ears, concerning this solemn business. Among the adults vague but well understood terms were used in conversing on this subject; and while it is certain that this grave concern was frequently the subject of guarded discussion in the two Monthly Meetings, still on the records no written reference to the subject is to be found.

RICHLAND, IOWA

Richland, Iowa, the oldest city in Keokuk County, sits in the far southeast corner of present-day Keokuk County. In 1840, it was on the border of the Indian lands to the west, in a portion referred to then as the "Old Strip." This small corner had been opened to pioneer settlement in 1838 following the Second Black Hawk purchase of 1837. The town was officially laid out on June 19, 1841. It was as far west as white settlers could locate until 1843. In its early days it was known as "Frog Town," but the reason why isn't clear. One tale says it is because the frogs in the ponds and small water holes were the only music that could be heard. As for the name of Richland, a story says that after a torrential downpour and days of standing water, the sun came out and exposed the richness of the dried soil; hence the name "Richland."

Soon after George and Lydia's arrival, Lydia gave birth to their first child born in Iowa. Miles was born in Keokuk County on March 20, 1841. Another son, John Milton, was born in Richland in September of 1842.

In fall of 1842, another treaty, referred to as the "New Purchase," or the "Treaty of 1842," was signed with the Indians in which all Sauk and Fox territory west of the Mississippi was ceded to the United States government.

The "New Lands" – Iowa Territory

On May 1, 1843, per this treaty, the Sauk and Fox were to yield possession of all land east of the Red Rock Line. They were given three years to surrender the land west of the Red Rock Line. After that time, they agreed to leave and go to a reservation in Kansas.

The dividing line was called the "Red Rock Line" because it was very near the town of Red Rock. Red Rock had come to life as a trading post in 1842. It had four saw mills, a flour mill, a hotel, a general merchandise store, a drug store, book store, a doctor and a Methodist church. It existed until 1960, when the Corps of Engineers bought land for Lake Red Rock. Lake Red Rock was created in 1969, flooding over the former town of Red Rock and five others. It is the largest lake in Iowa, with its waters flowing over the top of six former pioneer towns.

In exchange, the Sauk and Fox received payments and annual annuities. Payments were made in money, merchandise, domestic animals and gifts. They were not paid the true value of the land and too often the provisions of contracts were not entirely carried out as agreed.

During the last week of April 1843, the eastern border of the New Purchase was lined with settlers who were ready to race for the best claims. The fastest horses were readied and the quickest runners chosen, all in preparation to swiftly lay claim to the richest territories. They anxiously awaited the gunshots that would signal the opening of the land. Soldiers were stationed to keep them back until the hour of midnight arrived on April 30. At midnight, precisely, signal guns were discharged by the dragoons. In a burst of exuberance, punctuated by shouts, whoops, and a contagious uproar, the crowd surged across the boundary. They carried torches, axes and hatchets, and used any and all methods to lay out claims as quickly as they could.

Between midnight and daybreak, a large portion of the eastern part of the New Purchase was settled. George staked claims on sections three (forty acres) and thirty-three (eighty acres) near Sigourney, Iowa, about twenty miles northwest of Richland. (See Figure 8).

The second new community of Friends in Iowa was formed at Pleasant Plain, about twenty-five miles northeast of Salem and only about 10 miles from Richland. Ezekiel and Dolly became members of this Meeting and attended the Friends Church at Rocky Run. Rocky Run was about four miles from Richland. Pleasant Plain became a Monthly Meeting on December 28, 1842.

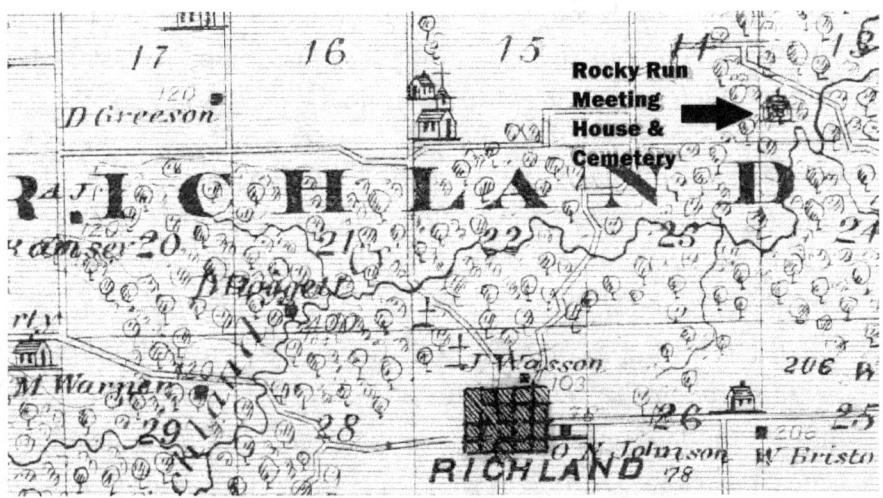

Figure 7: In this 1860 map, an arrow points to the location of Rocky Run Meeting house. Annotation of meeting house and cemetery added by author.

There is no trace of Rocky Run now. The church and adjoining cemetery fell victim to the plow many years ago and there is nothing to mark where it had been. Thankfully, some burials were documented by the Works Progress Administration in the 1930s. WPA employees compiled lists of cemeteries and burial records by searching church and cemetery offices, courthouse records and newspaper obituaries. By knowing where the cemetery was, we can better pinpoint where the church once stood. Per the WPA, the cemetery holds four graves; one of them being a grandson of Ezekiel. (Miles, son of Jeremiah; died February 17, 1854 at age nineteen.)

Quaker Eli Haworth also came to the region in 1840 from Vermilion County, Illinois. On May 18, 1846, he purchased the land that corresponds to the location on the map (See Figure 7) where the meeting house stood. Eli died on October 11, 1854 in Rocky Run, and is probably buried there as well.

Lydia's grandniece, Jessie (Hollingsworth) Schipfer, (of John Wesley, of Jeremiah, of Ezekiel) wrote a diary in 1935, affectionately called, "Jessie's Little Book," which gives us some special insight into the early days in Iowa Territory. It also helps to verify the location of the former Rocky Run Meeting house.[4] She wrote:

In 1840 the whole Hollingsworth family came to Keokuk County, Iowa. The whole family consisted of Ezekiel Hollingsworth, his wife and twelve children and their families. Jeremiah was a son of Ezekiel. Their forefather, Valentine Hollingsworth, came to this country with William Penn, so when Ezekiel's family settled in Iowa, it was fitting that all the Hollingsworths became members of the Friends Church at Rocky Run. The first minister of this church was John Howard, and another was John Y. Hoover, uncle of the former President, Herbert Hoover. To go to Rocky Run from the Hollingsworth home, one had to ford the Richland Creek, over which there were no bridges, and sometimes they had to cross in a boat when the water was high. But they went to

---

[4] "Jessie's Little Book," courtesy of Robert Lynn, the great grandchild of Jessie's sister Bessie (Hollingsworth) Kracht.

The "New Lands" – Iowa Territory

Meeting just the same.

When the Hollingsworths settled in Iowa, the state was passing through the earliest stages of pioneer life. They had come far away from the well-established reign of law and had entered a new country, where civil authority was still feeble and totally unable to afford protection and to redress grievances. The settlers lived here in Keokuk County for quite some time before there was a single officer of the law in the county. Each man's protection was the good will and friendship of those about him, and the thing any man might well dread was the ill will of the community, a force more terrible than the law. It was no uncommon thing in the early times for hardened men, who had no fear of jails and penitentiary, to stand in great fear of the indignation of a pioneer community.

One of the peculiar circumstances that surrounded the early life of the pioneers was a strange loneliness, consisting of a solitude which seemed almost to oppress them. Even so, cut off from the hope of aid in an emergency by the hundreds of miles of forest and plain that lay between them and the eastern population, they stood firm, trusting only in themselves for help. This self-reliance, constantly exercised through the whole of vigorous manhood and wrought into the character and habits of the young a singular mental robustness and confidence. They knew the meaning of fortitude. Success could not have failed them had the difficulty been ten times as great.

When the Hollingsworths settled in Iowa, their nearest neighbors were the Indians. Ezekiel and his family saw all the hardships incident to a pioneer life, in preparing a home for themselves and families. The first cabin the Hollingsworths lived in was a cross between hoop cabin and Indian bark hut. Jeremiah entered his claim in 1840 and obtained a patent deed from the Government, signed by James K. Polk. We still have the patent deed. Jeremiah was one of the Commissioners elected to organize the County, and he also served as a member of the Constitutional Committee that met at Iowa City in 1857. When Jeremiah went to Iowa City to fulfill his duties with this Committee, he rode horseback all the way from his farm home near Richland, commencing his journey on the twenty first of February. It took him two days to get there. The weather was very cold and his saddle was covered with sheep skins, one of which was also strapped around each of his legs. Now, that is the way they traveled in 1857.

Imagine, if you can, coming to a new country, building a home in the wilderness, with tall trees, hazel brush without end, and deer, elk, wildcats, foxes, wolves and snakes of all kinds, especially rattlesnakes. But this wilderness was not to remain for long. It is estimated that before nightfall of the first of May 1843, there were one thousand immigrants along what was called the Old Strip in Keokuk County, ready to cross over the line and stake their claims, the Indians having left the county. Around Rocky Run, May Day was a memorial to the first settlers for many years.

The wife (Anna) of the John Howard that Jesse wrote about is buried at Rocky Run Cemetery.

Keokuk County began organization in 1844, splitting off from Washington County. After the passing of the Treaty of 1842, land in Keokuk County became available to buy once it had been surveyed. Until then, a pioneer chose his spot and laid claim to it until such time as it became available to buy. Once available for purchase, if a claim wasn't bought, someone else could buy it or the person on the claim could run afoul with the government.

In 1846, all the land in Keokuk County became available for purchase from the government at the land office in Fairfield, Iowa. The sales were cash only on the State Bank of Missouri or coin. The cost was 1.25 per acre and the sale continued for two days. About 120 people purchased land over the two-day period.

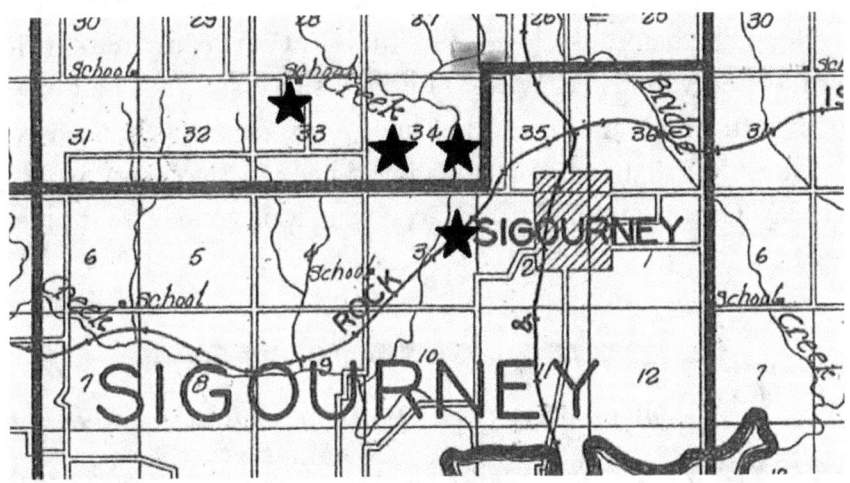

Figure 8: The stars denote George's government land purchases; forty acres each. Today Legion Park is located on part of his former land holdings in section three. Part of the Pleasant Grove Cemetery is now located on his eastern holdings on section thirty-four.

George was among them, as well as Eli Haworth and Lydia's brother Jeremiah. This was the only public sale of lands held for Keokuk County. George purchased his claims on sections three and thirty-three near Sigourney, Iowa. He later purchased land on section thirty-four.

Keokuk County's first election was held in April 1844 in Richland. Jeremiah Hollingsworth was elected one of three County Commissioners. A three-man commission was charged with locating the county seat. The men chose a site one mile from the geographic center of the county and named it Sigourney, after poetess Mrs. Lydia (Huntley) Sigourney. The people of Richland were opposed to this, as they felt the county seat should be located in the center of the population distribution rather than the geographical center.

A long, drawn out "county seat war" turned into a hotly contested and bitter dispute in the years to come. George was heavily involved in the effort to keep the county seat at Sigourney, Iowa, lobbying before the legislature in Iowa City in July 1845 with five other individuals. They were initially successful, but had only won a battle and not the war. The county seat was moved to Lancaster until 1856, when it was moved back to Sigourney, where it is today. George and Lydia, however, were long gone by that time.

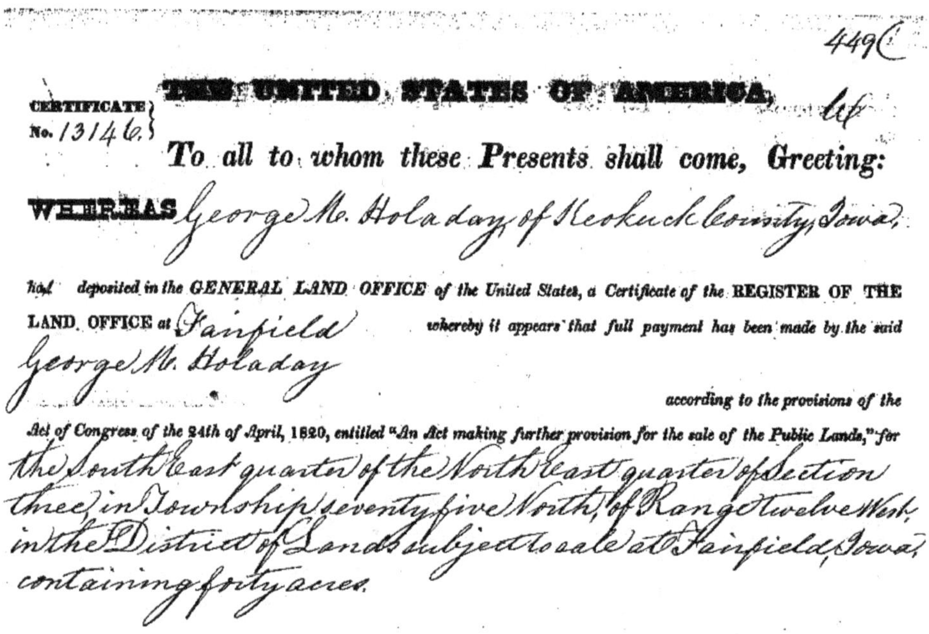
449 C

CERTIFICATE No. 13146. THE UNITED STATES OF AMERICA,

To all to whom these Presents shall come, Greeting:

WHEREAS George M. Holaday of Keokuck County, Iowa,

has deposited in the GENERAL LAND OFFICE of the United States, a Certificate of the REGISTER OF THE LAND OFFICE at Fairfield whereby it appears that full payment has been made by the said George M. Holaday according to the provisions of the Act of Congress of the 24th of April, 1820, entitled "An Act making further provision for the sale of the Public Lands," for the South East quarter of the North East quarter of Section three, in Township seventy five North, of Range twelve West, in the District of Lands subject to sale at Fairfield, Iowa, containing forty acres.

Figure 9: Land deed from purchase on section three in Keokuk County in 1846. (Bottom most star in Sigourney map on page 49)

On May 13, 1844, the Board of County Commissioners, which included Jeremiah Hollingsworth, met in Richland, Iowa. One of the items of business they conducted was to district the county into eighteen road districts and appoint supervisors. George was appointed supervisor of district four. They also chose the first Grand and Petit Juries and George was selected to be a petit juror. During the July term, George was granted a payment of $14 – 2023 equivalent of about $560 - for his role as a road commissioner.

On August 5, 1844, at age twenty-six, George was elected Sheriff of Ridge Precinct, which was just to the south of Sigourney.

On July 31, 1845, there was a meeting of the Keokuk County Temperance Society held at the courthouse in Sigourney. Sixty-eight individuals signed a pledge that read, "We, the undersigned, by hereto setting our names, pledge our sacred honor, each to the other, that we will abstain from all intoxicating drink as a beverage." George and Jeremiah were among the signatures, as well as Elias Hollingsworth, a son of Ezekiel.

Lydia's father, Ezekiel Hollingsworth, passed away about 1844. Unfortunately, no records have yet been located as to when he died, nor where he is buried. I believe he was likely buried at Rocky Run. We only know of his death because his widow returned east, creating Quaker records, and married again.

Dolly is next found in the Bloomingdale (Bloomfield) Indiana Monthly Meeting records of October 15, 1845, awaiting her certificate from the Pleasant Plain Monthly Meeting. At the next Monthly Meeting, her certificate had arrived from Pleasant Plain, dated September 24, 1845. Dolly and her husband-to-be, Mahlon Stephenson, were "left at liberty to accomplish their marriage" once her certificate arrived. They were wed on November 13, 1845 at the Rocky Run Meeting House in Parke County, Indiana.

Unfortunately, Mahlon died on January 15, 1846, just a few

months after their wedding. I have not yet found any further records for Dolly. She had lost three husbands and was a widow again at age fifty-three.

George and Lydia would have four more children while in Keokuk County: Caroline, born on November 27, 1844, twins Emma and Ellen on August 16, 1846, and William on March 25, 1848.

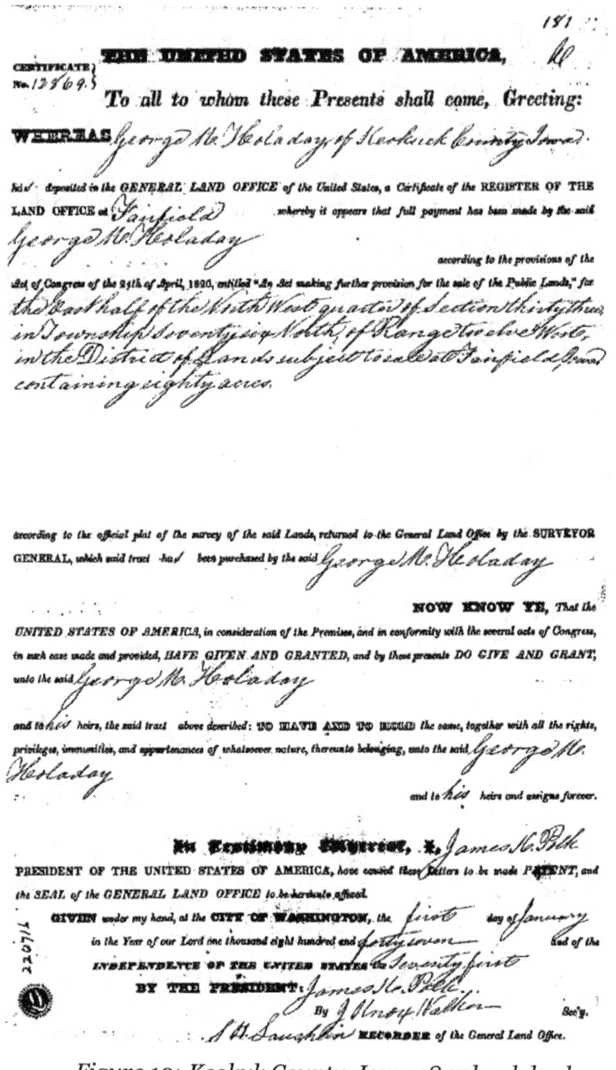

181

THE UNITED STATES OF AMERICA,

CERTIFICATE No. 12869.

To all to whom these Presents shall come, Greeting:

WHEREAS George M. Holaday of Keokuck County Iowa

has deposited in the GENERAL LAND OFFICE of the United States, a Certificate of the REGISTER OF THE LAND OFFICE at Fairfield whereby it appears that full payment has been made by the said George M. Holaday according to the provisions of the Act of Congress of the 24th of April, 1820, entitled "An Act making further provision for the sale of the Public Lands," for the East half of the North West quarter of Section thirty three in Township seventy six North, of Range twelve West, in the District of Lands subject to sale at Fairfield Iowa containing eighty acres.

according to the official plat of the survey of the said Lands, returned to the General Land Office by the SURVEYOR GENERAL, which said tract has been purchased by the said George M. Holaday

NOW KNOW YE, That the UNITED STATES OF AMERICA, in consideration of the Premises, and in conformity with the several acts of Congress, in such case made and provided, HAVE GIVEN AND GRANTED, and by these presents DO GIVE AND GRANT, unto the said George M. Holaday and to his heirs, the said tract above described: TO HAVE AND TO HOLD the same, together with all the rights, privileges, immunities, and appurtenances of whatsoever nature, thereunto belonging, unto the said George M. Holaday and to his heirs and assigns forever.

In Testimony Whereof, I, James K. Polk PRESIDENT OF THE UNITED STATES OF AMERICA, have caused these Letters to be made PATENT, and the SEAL of the GENERAL LAND OFFICE to be hereunto affixed.

GIVEN under my hand, at the CITY OF WASHINGTON, the first day of January in the Year of our Lord one thousand eight hundred and forty seven and of the INDEPENDENCE OF THE UNITED STATES the Seventy first

BY THE PRESIDENT: James K. Polk

By J. Knox Walker Sec'y.

S. H. Laughlin RECORDER of the General Land Office.

Figure 10: Keokuk County, Iowa 1847 land deed

CHAPTER 4
CALIFORNIA GOLD RUSH

When gold was found at Sutter's Mill in Coloma, California on January 24, 1848, it began a chain of events that would alter the course of history. Approximately 300,000 people would flock to California during the Gold Rush, about half arriving by sea and half overland.

The greatest number came in 1849, hence the term "49'ers." The gold discovery was a huge boon for the state of California, but had a severely negative impact on the Native Americans. Tens of billions of dollars in today's money was made in the Gold Rush, and some became fabulously wealthy. All too many, however, barely earned enough to pay their way. Those who got in early fared the best.

In August of 1848, the *New York Herald* reported the discovery of gold and in December 1848, United States President James K. Polk confirmed it in an address to Congress. The excitement from coast to coast was palpable. San Francisco, with a population of just 1,000 in 1848, swelled to 25,000 by 1850. Gold fever swept the nation, prompting men to borrow money, sell their homes and businesses, and deplete their life savings to reach California. Very few of them ever gained anything and the majority lost everything.

The problem for many was getting there. To get there from the east coast by ship took at least four months. The most popular overland trail was the California Trail. Any trail presented its share of dangers; accidents, cholera, illness, theft. Many women who traveled the trails with their husbands became widows before ever arriving. Even in California, their husbands were killed all too often in mining accidents and by disease.

As newspapers overflowed with tales of the gold to be found in California, an abundance of books, articles, pamphlets and guides were written and distributed. George found himself caught up in the excitement, and soon, his dreams began to crystallize into a tangible plan. He undoubtedly immersed himself in all available literature about California before resolving to join the westward-bound pioneers.

It's intriguing to ponder what Lydia thought of her husband's forthcoming scheme, especially with the responsibility of seven children resting on her shoulders. She would have certainly known the journey was a dangerous one, and that George might not make it back home. If she could have known it would be three years before he returned, I wonder if she would have agreed to it, although maybe he didn't give her a choice in the matter.

Daniel Toole, Jr., a "49'er," sent a letter about a California gold mining town to the *St. Joseph Weekly Gazette,* saying, "Unless the people become more civilized than they are at present, the Lord will doubtless sweep them speedily from the face of the earth... Great indeed is the excitement for gold. The majority of the people that live in this country have left their farms and families, sacrificing ease and comfort for the sake of obtaining gold."

GEORGE HEADS WEST

George left Keokuk County, Iowa on the 230-mile trip to St. Joseph, Missouri with ox teams in March of 1850. By this time, St. Joseph was one of the busiest cities in the country. Every item needed was for sale in St. Joseph, often at exaggerated prices. Every steamboat brought in merchant supplies to be sold to the emigrants who would lay out their life savings before they taking their lives in their hands for the hazardous trip across the plains.

The westward journey from the Great Plains had to begin in spring, once the grasses were sufficiently grown that they could feed the livestock. A pioneer could not bring enough feed with them and would be dependent on the land. It was imperative that the journey be completed before the snow came on the Sierra Nevada.

George would have spent some time in St. Joseph fully preparing his outfit for the journey and finding a wagon train to join. It is not known who accompanied George from Iowa, if anyone, nor which wagon train he joined, but he did not forgo it alone. There were too many dangers and difficulties on the trail and encounters with Indians still occurred. Pioneers needed the help of others in many situations, such as fording water crossings and getting wagons up and down inclines, as well as for protection.

It is estimated that at least 50,000 emigrants crossed the plains in 1850. It was a dry year, however, with almost double the number of travelers on the trail as the previous year. It suffered seriously from a lack of grass and good water.

About April 8, 1850, the first westbound wagon trains were leaving St. Joseph. Once the wagon trains rolled out, for miles, all the eye could see were long trains of wagons with their white covers. As they slowly ambled along, some rode alongside on horseback while most walked.

It was common for a traveler to join and leave various trains along the journey. Some large trains broke up into smaller ones. I suspect George either joined a smaller train from the beginning, or joined one later, as he arrived in California quickly compared to how long it took a large train.

Independence and St. Joseph, Missouri were the last towns on the frontier facing the Rockies. The Independence and St. Joseph roads came together at a point west of modern-day Marysville, Kansas, where they joined the Oregon and California Trails. Upon arriving at the convergence point in 1850, one pioneer noted, "Finally, when the two roads came together, and the army which had crossed the Missouri River at St. Joseph joined our army - it appeared to me that none of the population had been left behind. It seemed to me that I had never seen so many human beings before in all my life."

A multitude of ailments plagued travelers on the trail, ranging from minor inconveniences like diarrhea and colds, to deadly threats such as cholera, transmitted through tainted water sources. The hazardous conditions compounded as human and animal waste, refuse, and carcasses often contaminated nearby water supplies. Children were particularly vulnerable, with diphtheria emerging as the leading cause of death among them. Exhaustion and malnutrition rendered many pioneers susceptible to a host of other diseases, including typhoid, dysentery, malaria, food poisoning and scurvy. Additionally, outbreaks of measles, mumps and smallpox further compounded the challenges faced on the journey.

Accidents with livestock and firearms injured and killed many, yet others drowned in water crossings. Wagon accidents were common and of children who were injured or killed, it often involved falling under the wheels of a moving wagon. Thousands of pioneers were buried alongside the wagon trails and even underneath the trail itself. The latter was done to prevent animals from digging up the body. It is estimated that about five percent of those who undertook the journey died before arriving.

Every night the members of the trains camped out. Once a suitable campsite was found, the pioneers would "circle their wagons." This was done to better control the livestock, as well as for security reasons. Although Indian attacks were not common, some did occur and a wagon train in a straight line was a much easier target. Small wagon trains were also more susceptible to attack. Some of the attacks were for a wrong perpetuated on the Indians by a prior train, so no wagon train felt entirely safe from possible Indian attack. More often than not, however, Indians helped the pioneers. They ran ferries, helped with livestock and engaged in trading.

As the wagon trains made their way farther west, the challenges of the journey they'd undertaken began to show themselves. On the plains, they encountered violent thunderstorms, hail and heavy rains. Wagons broke down and any number of equipment problems arose. There was no wood to burn for fires, so they burned buffalo dung. Water became scarce and the livestock became tired pulling heavy loads. Emigrants often threw belongings along the side of the trail to lighten the load. The alkali swamps and springs poisoned and killed people, as well as livestock. No grass grew on the treeless plains, so there was no sustenance for the animals. In the far west there were long stretches without any water, grass or wood.

In a long advice article in the *St. Joseph Weekly Gazette* on April 5, 1850, the following advice was offered:

> *There is near these springs one or more sloughs, the deadly nature of whose waters is sufficiently marked by the numerous skeletons of stock lying around them. Keep guards out with your stock to prevent their approaching*

any other water but that in the springs. Leaving the spring near sundown, move on quietly all night for Carson's River; let none of your stock wander off from the train, as numbers of the Digger Indians infest the road all night to kill or drive off such animals as are left behind. Many wells have been sunk by the famishing emigrants along the road through this dreary desert, but the water is all salt as brine, and should not be used for man or beast as it only increases thirst. It may be possible that after having driven within eight or twelve miles of Carson's River, some of the stock will be unable to draw the wagons further on account of the heavy sands. Should this be the case, do not be alarmed or flurried in the least; leave several persons with the wagons and drive all the stock on to the river, when after grazing a day and night they will be able to return and bring up the wagons without difficulty.

The journey from St. Joseph to California was about 1600 miles. George arrived in Placerville, California in mid-June 1850, so his travel time was just over two and a half months. This was a daily average of about twenty-one miles per day, compared to a large train's average of about fifteen miles per day.

He worked the mines for at least several months, but, like so many others, was not successful in finding enough gold to justify the hard work of gold mining. He wasn't ready to give up on California yet, though. He soon learned there was money to be made in other endeavors.

On September 9, 1850, California became the thirty first state. The large influx of population during the Gold Rush hastened California's admittance to the Union.

TRINITY RIVER GOLD MINES

George went to San Francisco with a company of men in March 1851 with the intention of going to the new gold mines at Trinity River to the north. About four days after starting out, their vessel was wrecked and they were forced to return to San Francisco. From there they went to Sacramento, where George bought a wagon and a yoke of cattle and returned to Trinity River.

Apparently, gold didn't "pan out," and he and his company came up with a different plan – horse stealing. They hired a band of about fifty Indians to help steal fifty head of horses and mules from a coral owned by a Mr. Peasley and a Mr. Lockhart on Trinity River.

When the theft was discovered on the morning of April 21, 1851, eleven men followed on foot in pursuit, but seven turned back after encountering hostile Indians, believed to have been sent back to kill pursuers. The other four continued, later encountering a kindly settler who furnished them with provisions and horses. After they continued their journey, they were attacked by a party of Indians said to be numbered from fifty to one hundred, and a battle ensued. The pursuers claimed to have killed and scalped thirteen of the Indians.

The pursuers continued and on April 27, 1851, the animals were discovered grazing in a secluded area near Ide's Ranch, near Antelope Creek, in modern day Red Bluff, California.[5] As the pursuers entered the nearby chaparral to investigate, they were fired upon, but no one was hit. The first shot was attributed to George.

---

[5] Today "Ide's Ranch" is William B. Ides Adobe State Historic Park in Red Bluff, California. William B. Ide was a surveyor, miner, treasurer, district attorney, deputy clerk and judge. He also wrote the proclamation that established the short-lived California Bear Republic in 1846.

Another man, J. Spafford of Ohio, bolder than George, rose with his gun levelled, and was shot dead. The next to fire was John Emory, known as "Sailor Tom." He was also immediately shot dead. Both were scalped.

George successfully escaped, but was suspected to have been wounded. Years later, census documents would say that George was blind in his left eye. Whether he had always been blind in his left eye, or if it was a result of this injury, is unknown. A fourth thief escaped without injury. The camp was well stocked with provisions, cooking utensils, seven riding saddles, a pack of cards and "Lorenzo Dow."

Lorenzo Dow (1777 – 1834) was a popular, albeit eccentric, American evangelist and preacher. He attracted great crowds when he spoke; shouting, crying, begging, even screaming during his speeches. He was essentially a Methodist in doctrine. He wrote at least six works. It is assumed that the reference to "Lorenzo Dow" meant that one of those works was found in the camp.

The horse theft never catching up to him, George returned to Sacramento, California where he hired men to cut and bale wild oats in Napa Valley. They cut some 200 tons with an old-fashioned scythe, baled it and shipped it across the Suisun Bay and up the river to Sacramento. He owned half of a feed and sale stable with James Buckner on J. and Twelfth Streets. What hay they could not use they hauled to the gold mines and sold.

THE SQUATTER "HOLLIDAY"

In the fall of 1851, George set up a ranch on the south side of the Sacramento River six miles below Colusa, and about sixty miles north of Sacramento, which was then heavily timbered. He hired men to cut large quantities of wood, which he sold to steamers at eight dollars per cord. He assumed it was government land and he and about two hundred settlers laid claim to land in the area.

Figure 11: Sacramento, California, 1849 at the foot of J Street. *Drawn by G.V. Cooper on December 20, 1849. Library of Congress. Image in the public domain.*

George involved himself in politics as a Whig. At the Colusa County Convention held at the Colusa House Hotel on May 22, 1852, he was elected to constitute a county committee along with four other men. Delegates were appointed to attend the Whig State Convention to be held on the first Monday in June 1852. The Whig Party, founded in 1833 by Henry Clay, was a political party that existed in the United States during the mid-19th century. It consisted of those opposed to President Andrew Jackson and pulled together former members of the National Republican Party, the Anti-Masonic Party and disaffected Democrats. It collapsed in 1854 and George later became a Republican.

In 1851, squatter advocates pushed the California Land Act through Congress, subjecting all Mexican land grant claims to legal review by an appointed Land Commission. Ostensibly created to bring clarity to the legal morass, the act effectively put the grants into play, opening the door to a host of American swindlers and land sharks.

In fall of 1852, George was notified he must leave his Colusa ranch and the land, as it was Mexican grant land on the Larkin claim. George and the other settlers disagreed with the validity of a Mexican land grant and threatened to resist anyone who tried to take possession of it under a Spanish title.

The Larkin claim was a 44,364-acre Mexican land grant in present day Glenn and Colusa Counties. In 1844 it was given to the children of Thomas O. Larkin; Francesco, Caroline and Sophia, by Governor Manuel Micheltorena. Thomas O. Larkin, consul of the United States at Monterey, was unwilling to become a Mexican citizen, and thus could not obtain a direct land grant. In 1844, Larkin applied for the naturalization of three of his children and a land grant for them. Governor Micheltorena, heavily in debt to Larkin, complied. Two days after the children were naturalized, they received the grant. With the cession of California to the United States following the Mexican-American War, the 1848 Treaty of Guadalupe Hidalgo provided that the land grants would be honored. As required by the Land Act of 1851, a claim for Rancho Larkin's Children was filed with the Public Land Commission in 1852, and the grant was patented to Francisco Larkin, Caroline Ann Larkin, and Sophia Adelaide Larkin in 1857.

A Dr. Stoddard purchased 1,500 acres of land on the Larkin claim, which comprised the area where George and the others had settled. Being aware of the fact that George was still cutting the timber, he applied for a perpetual injunction to stay waste in the cutting of the timber. The United States District Court for the Northern District of California granted the injunction in May 1853.

Dr. Stoddard went to George's ranch and claimed ownership rights to the property. His wish was to take possession of the land.

His request was adamantly refused.

About 100 settlers gathered and elected George "Captain" and they determined they would force Dr. Stoddard out. George agreed to accomplish the task with a picked lot of men, and at midnight, they marched to the house of John Fitch, where Dr. Stoddard was staying.

George posted guards of four men at each door and window with instructions to allow no one to pass in or out. He took four more men and called to Mr. Fitch, who knew his voice and allowed them inside, although not yet knowing why they were there.

George and his men entered Dr. Stoddard's room. At first Dr. Stoddard appeared to be ready to fight, but quickly realized he was outnumbered.

They informed him that they were there to remove him, and assured him that not one hair of his head would be touched. The men took Dr. Stoddard and his belongings to the river bank. At this point, Dr. Stoddard was "the worst scared man you ever saw." He begged to be kept there until morning.

A vote was taken from the crowd and the overwhelming opinion was that Dr. Stoddard should be put over the river into Sutter County, which was a dense thicket inhabited by wild animals and grizzly bears. Dr. Stoddard survived the night, his only company the mosquitos, and the next morning went aboard the steamer, *Sutter*, returning to San Francisco. He immediately reported the matter to United States Deputy Marshal Douglass in San Francisco, California.

Marshal Douglass went to Colusa on May 21, 1853, for the purpose of serving summons to several parties on the Larkin claim, including George, to appear in court and show cause, if any, why injunctions should not be issued to stop them from committing waste. He sent several messages trying to explain his mission and that he only wished to discharge his duty as an officer. When he did not get the desired result of their resignation after two days, he went to them, against the advice of his friends.

He found about forty to fifty settlers "carousing together" and "making merry with liquor." They also had a fattened calf that they said they'd "appropriated" from a dead land speculator. He learned that a meeting had been held and resolutions passed to prevent, by force, his serving the summons.

He tried to reason with them but his attempts to do so failed. He was told in no uncertain terms that if he attempted to serve any papers, he would be lynched. He decided the risk was too great, so he left and boarded the steamer *Marysville*.

He learned that the steamer would be stopping at George's wood yard to pick up wood. He put the summons in an envelope and when the boat stopped, he went ashore. He told George that he had a letter from George's friends up the river. George opened the envelope and found that he had been duped. He had been served a summons. Marshal Douglass commenced in reading it aloud.

This infuriated George, and he immediately jumped on the woodpile, seizing a piece and telling the marshal that he would have to kill him first. While swinging the board at the marshal's head, it hit the marshal on the hand, arm and shoulder, knocking him down the riverbank. Marshal Douglass quickly returned to the boat as George went inside and grabbed his revolver. As George approached for a renewed assault, the boat captain interfered and George desisted. The boat soon left and Marshal Douglass went to San Francisco to obtain arrest warrants for George and other ringleaders.

After the marshal's departure, the squatters burned down Dr. Stoddard's property, which was said to be at least one house. Some of the squatters departed, but the ones that remained were determined. They said they would surrender only with their lives and would protect their claims with force of arms. The *Weekly Placer Herald* reported that they were "western men and well-armed," and if they would unite together, it could be "revolution or civil war."

In early June, tensions were high with the settlers believing that a force of United States troops would be sent to enforce the injunction against cutting timber. The overall sentiment of the settlers was not so much about the timber issue, but rather, of being evicted from their land claims. In short, they didn't believe in the legality of the Mexican land claim. They were not entirely wrong; there were indeed "gray" areas in the law. The bigger issue was *how* they went about holding on to their claims.

A scathing article was published in the *Daily Alta California* on May 28, 1853 that asked, "Will this band of lawless land thieves be permitted to maintain their attitude of defiance towards the United States Government?" Their alarm was apparent when it was also said, "Unless this band of outlaws be at once broken up, they will obtain a political formidableness, for there are demagogues enough who will espouse their cause, provided that political or party capital can be made out of it." They said the settlers were "a band of desperadoes whose hand is against every man, and who are to be brought into obedience to the law."

George was indicted for "assaulting an officer of the United States while in discharge of his duty." Several weeks later, on June 20, 1853, Marshal Douglass and officers North, Nugent and Andrew McKenzie, returned to arrest George and he was taken to San Francisco and jailed without incident.

He initially pleaded not guilty but changed his plea to guilty. On June 24, 1853, he was sentenced to pay a fine of $300. The *Daily*

Alta California reported that, "The punishment is a very light one for so grave an offence."

George sold his ranch, the four hundred cords of wood he had on hand, and all of his livestock. Upon his release from jail in California, he returned to Iowa.

> **LAW REPORT.**
> U. S. District Court.—O. Hoffman, jr., Judge.—June 24. *The U. S.* vs. *George H. Holladay.*—Prisoner withdrew plea of not guilty and plead guilty. The court sentenced said Holladay to pay a fine of $300, and to stand committed until said fine be paid.

Figure 12: *"Law Report," June 25, 1853*, Daily Alta California. Courtesy of the California Digital Newspaper Collection, Center for Bibliographic Studies and Research, University of California, Riverside, http://cdnc.ucr.edu.

> THE SQUATTER HOLLIDAY, who made the furious assault upon the person of U. S. Marshal Douglass a short time since in the neighborhood of Colusi, was brought down to this city last night in company of the U. S. Marshal and officers North, Nugent, and Andrew McKenzie. They stole a march upon him and the whole affair was conducted with the nicest judgment and tact. An amusing incident oc-

Figure 13: *"The Squatter Holliday," June 21, 1853*, Daily Alta California. Courtesy of the California Digital Newspaper Collection, Center for Bibliographic Studies and Research, University of California, Riverside, http://cdnc.ucr.edu.

CHAPTER 5
ADAIR COUNTY, IOWA

After George's return from California, he convinced Lydia that they should go west to Kanesville, Iowa (present day Council Bluffs, Iowa), where the government was buying land from the Indians. Council Bluffs was a quickly growing town, first named Trader's Point in 1824. It was renamed Kanesville in 1846 after Thomas L. Kane. He had helped negotiate federal permission for the Mormons to use Indian land along the Missouri River for their winter encampment of 1846-1847. The town was renamed once more after a site about twenty miles to its north, where the Lewis and Clark Expedition members had sat in council with the Otoe Tribe on bluffs near the Missouri River.

A writing from Alice Grethel (Edwards) Stotts, George and Lydia's great granddaughter, tells a tale about George and Lydia's move west from Keokuk County to Adair County. This story is in the FamilySearch library in Salt Lake City on microfilm. It is a wonderful story, although it contains a great many errors. It was surely handed down from generation to generation and perhaps in the retelling, the information became garbled. Following are her words, although I have made edits and corrections.

George was of an adventuresome and restless nature and his wife was not always in agreement with his continual moving. When he decided to move further west in 1853 from Keokuk County and go to Kanesville (Council Bluffs) where the government was buying land from the Indians, and the town was growing rapidly and the government was establishing a school, she was in accord with this move, as she was very desirous of her children obtaining an education.

They set out in covered wagons in the wet, rainy summer of 1853. The normally small streams were wide and difficult to ford. The many lowlands were vast swamps. The rain fell upon them every day and one of the wagons broke a wheel. It took them over a week to travel from Keokuk County to a spot north of the present town of Fontanelle, near the Middle River. Late one afternoon they came to a clearing in the seemingly endless forest that covered most of Adair County at that time. George decided it was a likely place to camp overnight. The sun broke through the clouds and Mrs. Holaday set about spreading out rain-soaked garments and bedding to dry while George followed a small cloud of smoke he saw rising from amongst the trees to learn where he might obtain drinking water. He came to a log cabin, where one man was living alone. This man, name forgotten through the years, was discouraged and completely disgusted with Iowa in general and that place in particular. George pointed out the fine qualities of the trees and the land where it was cleared and it seems, sold himself on the idea of settling there. After an hour or two of argument and haggling, he bought the land to which the discouraged owner claimed ownership, or rather, traded a team and wagon for it.

George obtained a pail of water from the man and returned

to his campsite. He asked his wife what she would say if he told her that he had just traded for the land on which they were camping. She made no reply, but sat down on the wagon tongue and wept. Her disappointment passed, and after a few years, schools came to Adair County.

It is not known if this is exactly the place where they settled, but George soon built a double log cabin on section twenty-six, near the Middle River, in Adair County, in what would become Jefferson Township. It was said to be the best house in the county at the time, although there were few other families. The total population of Adair County the following year was 150 persons; 78 males and 72 females. In 2020, the population was 7,496. Adair County comprises 570 square miles.

Figure 14: Jefferson Township, Adair County, Iowa, 1875. An arrow points to Holaday's Post Office. A.T. Andreas Illustrated Historical Atlas of the State of Iowa. (Chicago, Ill.: Andreas Atlas Co., 1875)

The first to have made a settlement in Jefferson Township was William Alcorn in 1850, and he planted the first corn in 1852. Very few others came to the township until 1853. From 1853 onward, settlers slowly came into the township and the county alike, building their homes and establishing their farms.

George purchased a great deal of land, taking up farming and stock raising. He sowed the first wheat in Jefferson Township in 1854 and the first oats were sown by him (on section thirty-five) and John Febus (on section twenty-seven) in the spring of 1854.

In the fall of 1854, the first birth in Jefferson Township was George and Lydia's son Thomas Jefferson Holaday. It is said the township was named after him. Sadly, the child died at about one year of age in the fall of 1855. The son of William Alcorn, who was seven or eight years old in 1853, succumbed to a rattlesnake bite and was the first death in Jefferson Township. Both children were buried in the same pasture field on section twenty-six.

Adair County was established by the Iowa General Assembly on January 15, 1851. It was named in honor of John Adair, a prominent military figure in the War of 1812 and a governor of Kentucky. The office of county judge was created by an act of the General Assembly in 1851 and was the most important office in the county. The judge, assisted by a county prosecuting attorney and a sheriff, held what was termed county court, and transacted almost all the business that in modern times is done by the auditor, board of supervisors, circuit court and clerk of courts.

George was the first to occupy the position of county judge in Adair County, being elected in April 1854. The election was held in his home, now located on section thirty-five. The first officers chosen were Jacob Bruce, William McDonald and Robert Wilson, trustees; William Hollingsworth, clerk; and Jacob Bruce, road supervisor.

On May 6, 1854, the first meeting of the county court was held at George and Lydia's home. The only business before the court at that time was the granting of a marriage license to William Stinson and Elizabeth F. Crow. On May 8, 1854, George performed their marriage, the first marriage of Adair County, at the residence of William Alcorn.

In the July term, on July 3, 1854, George ordered that the county of Adair be divided into two election precincts, with the center line running north and south to be the dividing line. The east half was to be known as Harrison Precinct and the west half as Washington Precinct. He ordered that Alfred Jones, Thomas N. Johnson and Nathan Wooart be appointed township trustees of Washington precinct, Adair County, Iowa.

In the September term, on September 5, 1854, the first levy of taxes was made.

In January 1855, the General Assembly of Iowa appointed Elias Stafford of Madison County, George B. Hitchcock of Cass County, and John Buckingham of Page County as commissioners to locate the Adair County seat.

On April 27, 1855, the first two commissioners reported to Judge George Holaday that they had, on the 24th of that month, met and located the Seat of Justice and named it Summerset. It was to be located on the southwest quarter of section seventeen, township seventy-five north, range thirty-two west. The order was entered by Judge Holaday; the funds being supplied by Enos Lowe.[6]

---

[6] Enos Lowe (1804-1880) was a Quaker pioneer, medical doctor and business man who was among the original founders of Omaha, Nebraska. His brother Jesse was the first mayor of Omaha. Enos served as president of the Second Iowa Constitutional Convention. In 1853, he was appointed receiver of the United States

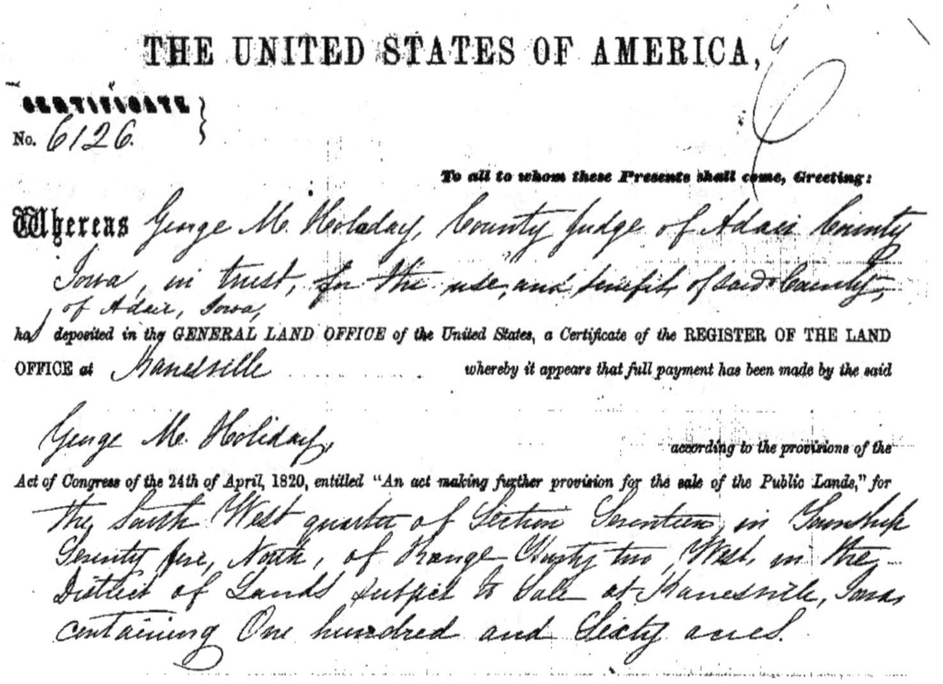

THE UNITED STATES OF AMERICA,

CERTIFICATE
No. 6126.

To all to whom these Presents shall come, Greeting:

Whereas George M. Holladay, County Judge of Adair County Iowa, in trust, for the use and benefit of said County, of Adair, Iowa, has deposited in the GENERAL LAND OFFICE of the United States, a Certificate of the REGISTER OF THE LAND OFFICE at Kanesville whereby it appears that full payment has been made by the said George M. Holliday, according to the provisions of the Act of Congress of the 24th of April, 1820, entitled "An act making further provision for the sale of the Public Lands," for the South West quarter of Section Seventeen, in Township Seventy five, North, of Range Thirty two, West, in the District of Lands subject to Sale at Kanesville, Iowa containing One hundred and Sixty acres.

Figure 15: George land purchase as Adair County Judge

On April 30, 1855, George, in his capacity as judge of Adair County, purchased 160 acres at a cost of $200 - 2023 equivalent of about $7k - at the land office in Kanesville, Iowa (Council Bluffs), to be held in trust for the use and benefit of Adair County.[7]

Along with prominent attorney Daniel M. Valentine, the county surveyor, and Abram Rutt, the town of Summerset was laid out. (Its name was changed to Fontanelle in 1857). It remained the county

---

Land Office at Council Bluffs, Iowa. In 1853, Enos, his brother Jesse, and several partners co-founded the Council Bluffs and Omaha Steam Ferry Company, which laid out the town site for Omaha west of the Missouri River. Enos became the first president of the Omaha Medical Society in Omaha in 1866. His connection to Fontanelle, Iowa is uncertain.

[7] In 1859, George filed a Quit Claim Deed on the land.

seat until 1875, when it was moved to Greenfield, Iowa.

Jefferson Township's post office was established in 1853, mainly to accommodate the emigrants to the golden shores of the Pacific during the great overland travel to California. It was named Holaday's Post Office when George was elected to the judgeship. On March 23, 1855, George was appointed Postmaster for the 1855-1856 term. Holaday's Post Office was discontinued in 1899, but bore that title until then. (See Figure 14)

In the July term, on July 3, 1855, a new township was established in congressional townships seventy-four and seventy-five, to be known as Grand River Township. Robert Wilson, Charles Wilson and William Swears were appointed trustees. Townships seventy-six and seventy-seven, ranges thirty-one, thirty-two and thirty-three were established under the name of Jefferson Township. Mahundry Hollingsworth, Samuel Miner and William Tingle were appointed trustees. Mahundry Hollingsworth was George's wife Lydia's brother.

It was also ordered that George be allowed $52.50 as salary for fifteen months as county judge from April 1, 1854 to July 1, 1855. (2023 equivalent of about $1,850). The county clerk, John Gibson, was allowed $62.50 as his salary for fifteen months. (2023 equivalent of about $2,200).

One of George's last orders as judge was that Joshua Chapman, recorder and treasurer of Adair County, was to be allowed $50 for his one year of service from August 1854 to August 1855. (2023 equivalent of about $1,750). Judge Leeper became the next county judge.

One of the last things George did in Jefferson Township was to assist with laying the foundation for the first schoolhouse.

It is not known what happened for George's judgeship to end

when it did, as it appears he did not finish his entire term. In 1915, it was written in the *History of Adair County* that, "He left here for Des Moines, whither he went to educate his children. He did not turn out well..."

The 1884 *History of Guthrie and Adair Counties* mysteriously said only, "After George's term of elected county judge, he left the county under a cloud."

The "cloud," I believe, was that he was having an affair. It's a fact that he engaged in an affair; however, the specifics of its early details are largely speculative on my part. I will leave it to you, dear reader, to come to your own conclusions.

In various records, this woman's name has been recorded as Elvira, Elmira and Alvira. I will refer to her as Elvira, as I believe this to be the accurate name.

On July 27, 1855, George, in his capacity as judge, signed off on a town lot land sale to "Elvira Collins." The deed says she was of Cass County, which is the county adjacent to Adair County to the west. This appears to be George's last act as county judge. She quickly resold the lot, at a loss, on August 6, 1855.

It is my belief that Elvira Collins may have become the family's domestic helper or nanny and may have moved in with them.[8] The family may have been living in or near Summerset, (Fontanelle) Iowa at the time, as George had purchased land there. Royce Bissell, a family historian, referred to the mistress as possibly being the "hired girl."[9] It wasn't uncommon for a family as large as theirs, with

---

[8] *Please note...* It is not at all certain that Elvira *Collins* was the woman with which George had an affair. The only thing that is certain is that her name was Elvira, or very similar.

[9] Royce Bissell was married to Mildred Eva Holaday, George & Lydia's great

the economic means that they had, to hire domestic help.

In 1856, Elvira Collins was on the state census, enumerated in June, in Fort Des Moines, Polk County, Iowa as a twenty-eight-year-old widow. This Iowa census marks the sole census record of her presence in the state. It is unknown whether she had lived here all along, had relocated from Cass County or relocated from Fontanelle.

George and Lydia are on the same census living in Adair County. By this time, they'd had another child, Orpha. She shows as "0" years old, so her birth was likely in May or June 1856. She died young and there are no further records for her. The only mention of her place of death is in an article in the *Greenfield Free Press* on July 13, 1911, where it says that she died as an infant while George and Lydia lived on the Middle River in Adair County. Her burial location remains unknown.

Soon after appearing on the Adair County census, George, Lydia and family moved to Des Moines, Polk County, Iowa.

FORT DES MOINES, POLK COUNTY, IOWA

On January 28, 1857, with the adoption of a city charter, the name of the county seat was changed from Fort Des Moines to Des Moines, the name it bears today. The population in 1857 was 3,800. The state capital was moved from Iowa City to Des Moines in October 1857. While George undoubtedly recognized opportunities in the burgeoning capital city, his motivations were likely multifaceted.

1857 was a year of great commercial depression, which brought

---

granddaughter. In 1980, he wrote a manuscript entitled, "The Other Side," which contained extensive family research. It was distributed among family members and is also at the Winterset, Iowa Public Library.

on a panic that caused disaster throughout the United States. Many pioneer business men were ruined and business enterprises of all kinds were brought to a standstill. It was caused by the declining international economy, over expansion of the domestic economy, as well as the bankruptcy of securities brokers who borrowed from eastern banks to finance their dealings in the stock and bond markets. It is referred to as the "Panic of 1857," and was the first financial crisis to spread rapidly throughout the United States, as well as being one of the most severe economic crises in United States history. Its trigger was when a New York division of the Ohio Life Insurance and Trust Company ceased making payments to investors because the cashier had embezzled its funds.

George and Lydia's tenth born child and fifth daughter, Pauline, was born on June 19, 1857 in Des Moines. Assuming Orpha had passed away by this time, Lydia now had eight children to tend.

On October 13, 1857, George was elected a justice of the peace for Lee Township in Des Moines. His term ran from 1857 to 1858. Lee Township was split off from Des Moines Township, comprising a large section of the east side of Des Moines as well as part of the south side. The 460-acre Iowa State Fairgrounds are in Lee Township, although the fair was not held on that location until 1886.

The Holaday family and Elvira were all residents of Des Moines now. It's conceivable that Elvira might have resided with them as a domestic aide. Alternatively, she might have lived independently, perhaps concealed from Lydia as she and George's affair continued.

Exactly how the relationship progressed is frustratingly puzzling, but the affair resulted in the birth of a son, George Washington Holaday, born on March 2, 1859. Elvira was thirty years old and George was forty-one.

The extent of Lydia's knowledge regarding the affair or the existence of the child remains shrouded in mystery. A reference in a single history book said only that George "left the country with another woman" - which is exactly what he did in 1860.

Figure 16: Des Moines Capitol, 1857-1886. *It was destroyed by fire in 1892. The Soldiers and Sailors Monument stands in its former place today. Image by Joseph P. Sharman. Library of Congress, from the Historic American Buildings Survey. Image in the public domain.*

Figure 17: The Demoine House, *a lively spot in Des Moines, built in 1855. Image by Joseph P. Sharman from* Beginnings: Reminiscences of Early Des Moines *by Tacitus Hussey, 1919. Image in the public domain.*

MISCELLANY. . .

While in Adair County, George purchased a patent, originally issued to Horace Billings in June 1848, for a "new and valuable fire and water proof material" from E.C. Sackett and Company. The deed was signed on January 1, 1856 at Holaday's post office. What George did with this patented material is unknown.

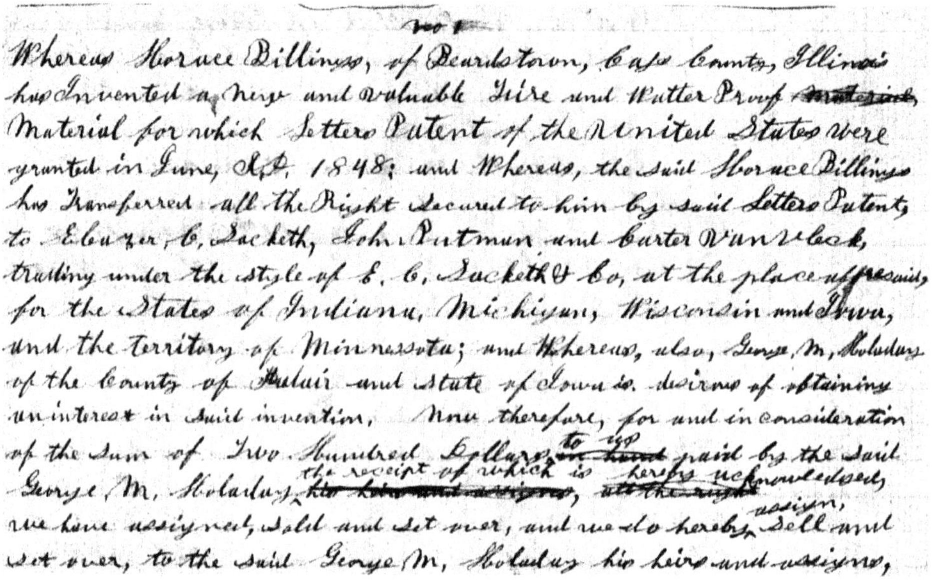

Whereas Horace Billings, of Beardstown, Cass County, Illinois
has Invented a New and valuable Fire and Watter Proof ~~material~~
Material for which Letters Patent of the United States were
granted in June, A.D. 1848; and Whereas, the said Horace Billings
has Transferred all the Right secured to him by said Letters Patent,
to Ebenezer C. Sackett, John Putman and Carter Van Vleck,
trading under the style of E. C. Sackett & Co, at the place aforesaid,
for the States of Indiana, Michigan, Wisconsin and Iowa,
and the Territory of Minnessota; and Whereas, also, George M. Holaday
of the County of Adair and State of Iowa is desirous of obtaining
an interest in said invention, Now therefore, for and in consideration
of the Sum of Two Hundred Dollars to us ~~in hand~~ paid by the said
George M. Holaday, the receipt of which is ~~his heirs and assigns~~, hereby acknowledged, ~~at the right~~
we have assigned, sold and set over, and we do hereby assign, sell and
set over, to the said George M. Holaday his heirs and assigns,

Figure 18: Adair County Historical Records, Recorder: Deeds, Book 1, page 40 (above) and 41 (below)

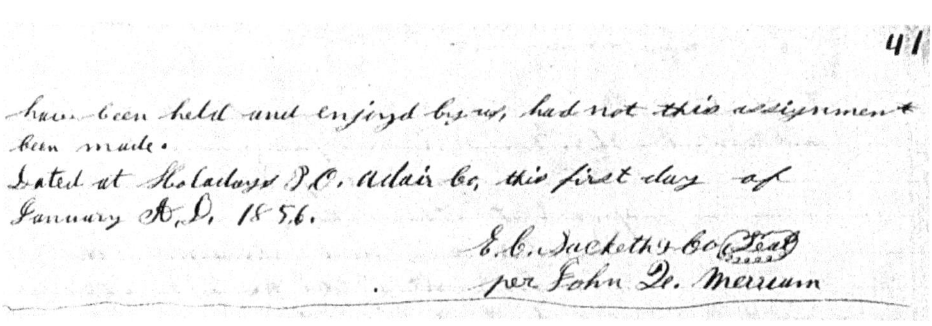

41

have been held and enjoyed by us, had not this assignment
been made.
Dated at Holadays P.O. Adair Co, this first day of
January A.D. 1856.
E.C. Sackett & Co (Seal)
per John D. Merriam

CHAPTER 6
WINTERSET, MADISON COUNTY, IOWA

In late 1858 or early 1859, George, Lydia and family left Des Moines and moved to Winterset in Madison County, Iowa. Winterset is about forty miles southwest of Des Moines and about forty miles southeast of Jefferson Township. It is not clear why they left Des Moines, nor why they chose Winterset for their new home. Winterset was laid out in 1849 and by 1860, the population was 915.

What comes to the minds of most in reference to Madison County is Robert James Waller's best-selling novel, *The Bridges of Madison County,* which was later adapted into a feature film and a musical. Built between 1870 and 1880, there were once nineteen covered bridges in the county, but today just six remain. All are listed on the National Register of Historic Places. Also of note is its distinction as the birthplace of actor John Wayne.

In 1850, Winterset was on an unbroken prairie, almost wholly destitute of trees, with a handful of cabins. By 1854, however, the town began to grow rapidly. In 1856, Judge John A. Pitzer built the "Pitzer House," which would become known as the St. Nicholas

Hotel. It was considered the finest hotel – and the largest - in southwestern Iowa, famed for its entertainment and hospitality. It was located at 101 W. Jefferson St., dominating the northwest corner of the town square. It was built with native limestone at a cost of $12,000. It was a large three-story stone building with a porch that covered the entrance and sidewalk for the entire length of the building. A number of other fine residences and businesses were built immediately after its construction.

Figure 19: St. Nicholas Hotel. *The man in front is unidentified.* Mueller, Herman A. (Ed.). (1915). History of Madison County Iowa and its People (Vol. I). Chicago, IL, USA: The S.J. Clarke Publishing Company. Image in the public domain.

Winterset's steady growth helped secure incorporation in April 1857. Soon after, though, in September, the Panic of 1857 hit Winterset hard, depreciating property values and nearly ruining every business man. With time, Winterset began a period of slow but steady growth.

George and Lydia owned and operated the St. Nicholas Hotel at some point. * In the western part of the building was the hotel kept by the Holadays and later by their son Samuel. The lower room of the eastern side had once been a saloon. The upper rooms were rented out; one to a law office and the other to the *Hawkeye Flag* newspaper – the only newspaper in Winterset. (It later became the *Madisonian*). The third floor contained the offices of the county judge, treasurer and recorder.

It was also a stage stop, carrying the mail as well as passengers. The stage was drawn up in front of the St. Nicholas each morning. In a paper written by George and Lydia's daughter Caroline, she described the arrival of the stage:

> *The pride of those stage drivers in making a rapid entry, and the peculiar crack and wielding of their whips and the masterful way of rounding corners was something only attained by long experience. Then they were also news carriers, anything that had happened in the outside world since they had left in the morning was quickly told, and eagerly listened to by the many by-standers who had congregated to witness the grand entry and hear the latest news.*

Figure 20: St. Nicholas Hotel. *Madison County Historical Society collection. Image in the public domain.*

In 1886, George Washington Carver (~1864 - 1943), one of the most prominent black scientists of the early twentieth century, was a cook at the St. Nicholas. Mr. Carver had been born into slavery in Missouri. In 1890, Carver started studying art and piano at Simpson College in Indianola, Iowa. His art teacher, Etta Budd, recognized Carver's talent for painting flowers and plants and encouraged him to study botany at Iowa State Agricultural College, now Iowa State University, in Ames. When he began there in 1891, he was the first black student at Iowa State.

The St. Nicholas was razed about 1918 and the Citizen's National Bank was built in its place. When Citizen's closed, the Farmer's & Merchant's State Bank took up residence and is now on the former location of the hotel.

George, among others, became involved in a lawsuit filed against Adair County in 1859. The individuals wanted payment for time spent as jurors. I am unclear as to why this culminated in a lawsuit. George's attorney was Daniel M. Valentine.

Daniel Mulford Valentine's (1830 – 1907) career started in Adair County, Iowa as a county land surveyor. After being admitted to the bar in 1858, he became the county attorney for Adair County. Daniel married Martha Root on June 26, 1855 in Fontanelle, Iowa. They moved to Kansas about 1860, and he became a member of the Kansas House of Representatives in 1862, a member of the Kansas State Senate in 1863 and 1864, and a justice on the Kansas Supreme Court from 1869 to 1893. George and Lydia's son Samuel would marry Martha's sister, Almyra, in 1863. Martha and Almyra's father was Azariah Root, Jr., who served as Adair County judge from 1861 to 1864.

Daniel kept a daily diary in which several references are made to George and the court case.

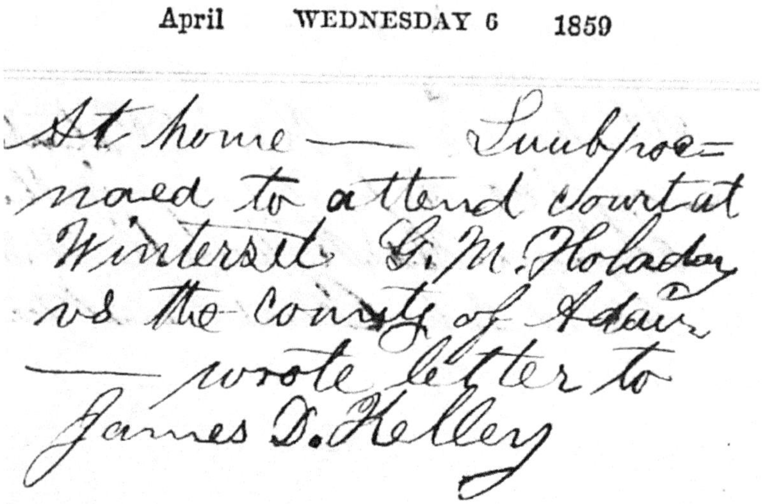

April WEDNESDAY 6 1859

At home — Subpoenaed to attend court at Winterset G. M. Holaday vs the county of Adair — wrote letter to James D. Kelley

Figure 21: April 6, 1859: "At home – Subpoenaed to attend court at Winterset. G.M. Holaday vs the county of Adair – wrote letter to James D. Kelley." *From Daniel M. Valentine's Diary, courtesy of Kansasmemory.org, Kansas State Historical Society.*

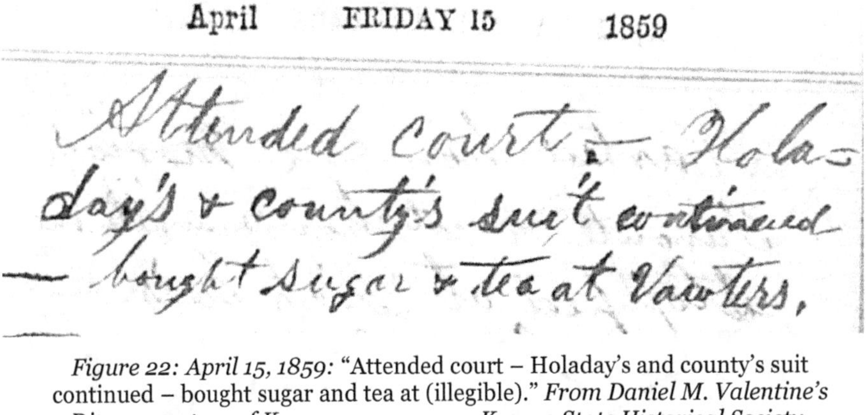

April FRIDAY 15 1859

Attended court — Holaday's & county's suit continued — bought sugar & tea at Vawters,

Figure 22: April 15, 1859: "Attended court – Holaday's and county's suit continued – bought sugar and tea at (illegible)." *From Daniel M. Valentine's Diary, courtesy of Kansasmemory.org, Kansas State Historical Society.*

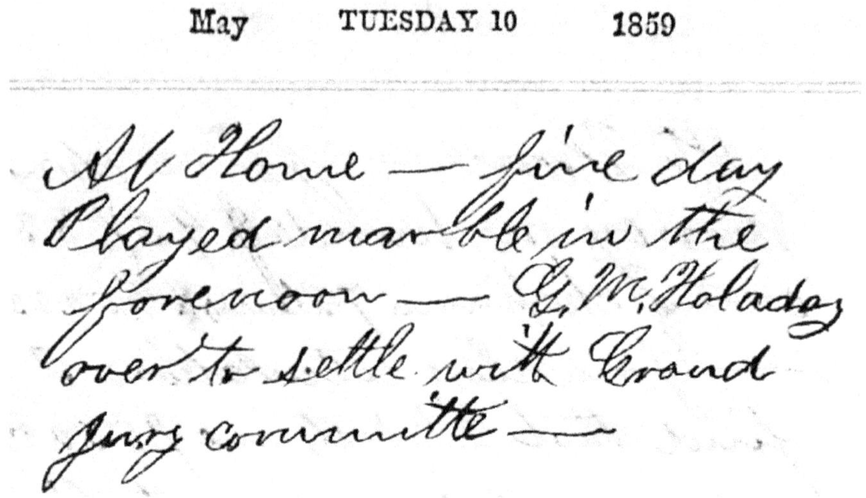

Winterset, Madison County, Iowa

May   TUESDAY 10   1859

Figure 23: May 10, 1859: "At Home - fine day. Played marbles in the forenoon - G.M. Holaday over to settle with Grand Jury committee." From Daniel M. Valentine's Diary, courtesy of Kansasmemory.org, Kansas State Historical Society.

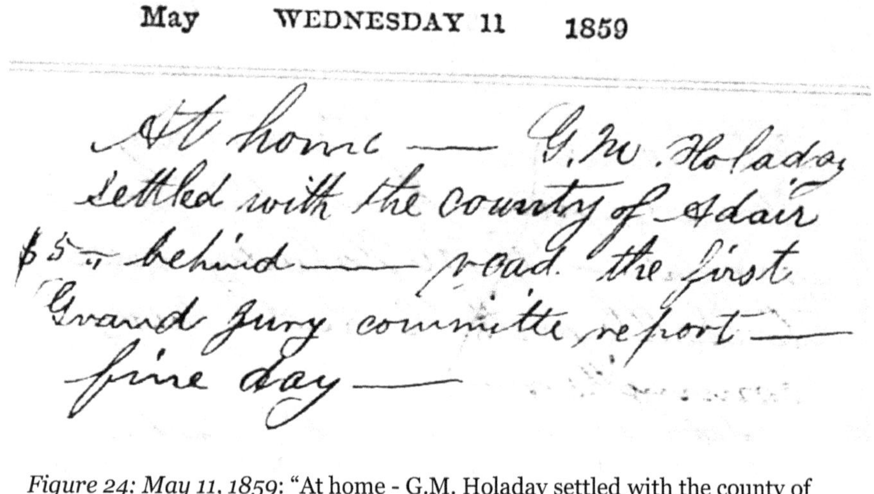

May   WEDNESDAY 11   1859

Figure 24: May 11, 1859: "At home - G.M. Holaday settled with the county of Adair $5 behind – read the first Grand Jury committee report - fine day." From Daniel M. Valentine's Diary, courtesy of Kansasmemory.org, Kansas State Historical Society.

George and Lydia's last-born child, a son they named Henry Delano, was born on April 10, 1860 in Winterset. George, Lydia and children, minus Orpha, all appear together on the 1860 Federal Census in Winterset. The report does not show any female home servants or the child born to George and Elvira.

It is not known where Elvira or she and George's son George W. were at this time, but I suspect they stayed back in Des Moines. Winterset was still a small town, with a population of 915 in 1860. In 1859, with an even smaller population, a single mother with a child would have been very conspicuous.

Daniel Mulford and Martha (Root) Valentine.
Image source for Martha's photo - Martha Sutton. Image source for Daniel – unknown.

* A land record bearing the date of November 25, 1865 shows Lydia purchasing one third of the lot the St. Nicholas sits on from Judge Pitzer and wife Elizabeth for what appears to be a curious sum of only $1.00. Whether George and Lydia owned any of the hotel lot(s) prior to this time is unknown.

Madison County has the greatest number of covered wooden bridges surviving in Iowa. The Holliwell Bridge is the longest, at 110 feet. It was built by Harvy P. Jones and George K. Foster at a cost of $1,180 in 1880. It was one of two bridges featured in *The Bridges of Madison County* movie.

Figure 25: The Holliwell Covered Bridge, built in 1880. George and Lydia's granddaughter Elizabeth Murray, along with friends, had a picnic just to the east of the bridge on August 29, 1901. It is still standing in its original location over the Middle River. It was featured in the Bridges of Madison County *movie. It was renovated in 1995 at a cost of $225,000.*

Historic American Engineering Record, C., Foster, G. K., Jones, H. P., Town, I., Marston, C. H., Federal Highway Administration, S. [...] Bennett, L., Elliott, J. E. B. & Lowe, J., photographer. (1968) Holliwell Bridge, Spanning Middle River at Holliwell Bridge Road (now bypassed) (changed from Spanning Middle River at county road), Winterset, Madison County, IA, 1968. *Retrieved from the Library of Congress, https://www.loc.gov/item/ia0440/ Image in the public domain.*

CHAPTER 7
PIKE'S PEAK GOLD RUSH

Figure 26: Prospector on Pike's Peak *by William H. Jackson. Library of Congress. Image in the public domain.*

Once again, wanderlust would propel George westward. This time, however, he went with his son Miles. In the years to come, George would make quite a name for himself in the West, never to return to Iowa. It is astonishing how he was able to establish himself in the positions of power that he did in the future considering what he now had in his past.

Sparked by the discovery of gold in the vicinity of Pike's Peak in present-day Colorado in 1858, the Pike's Peak Gold Rush was a short lived, but frenzied period of migration and prospecting.[10] Gold was never actually found on Pike's Peak, but the peak was the closest and most recognizable landmark near where it was found.

News of the discovery spread rapidly, triggering a massive influx of fortune seekers from across the United States and even from overseas. As many as 100,000 gold seekers rushed into the area. They became known as "59'ers," using the motto, "Pike's Peak or Bust!"

As prospectors flooded into the region, makeshift settlements and boomtowns sprang up almost overnight. These towns, such as Denver City, Boulder City, Breckenridge, South Park and Colorado City, soon became bustling centers of activity, with saloons, gambling halls and other businesses catering to the needs of the miners.

Life in the gold rush towns was rough, tough and often lawless. Prospectors faced numerous challenges, including harsh weather conditions, rugged terrain and conflicts with Native American tribes who inhabited the area.

News of Pike's Peak didn't escape the men of Winterset, Iowa. As with the rest of the nation, they followed the stories, read the newspapers and made their plans.

On April 4, 1860, George and Lydia sold 320 acres of Adair County land, netting $5,000 on its sale (2023 equivalent of $188k).

---

[10] Present day Colorado was still Kansas Territory in 1860.

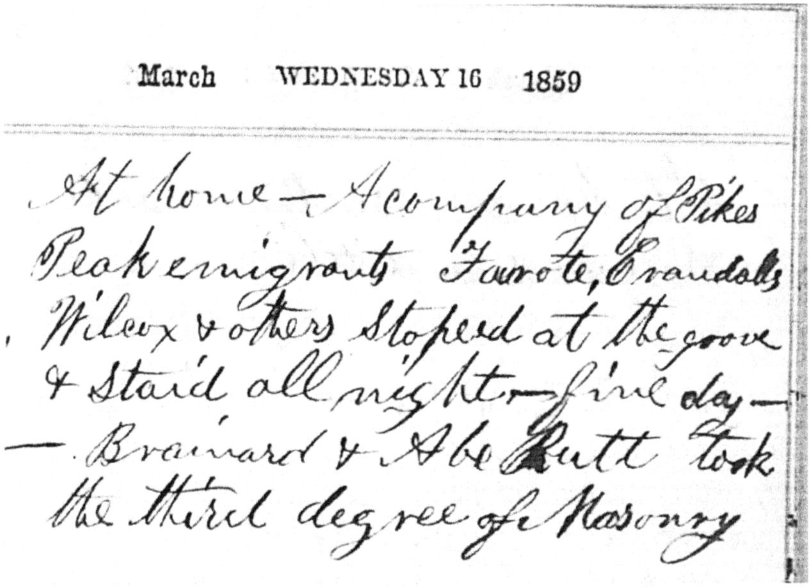

> March WEDNESDAY 16 1859
>
> *At home – A company of Pikes Peak emigrants Faurote, Crandall, Wilcox & others stoped at the grove & staid all night – fine day – Brainard & Abe Rutt took the third degree of Masonry*

Figure 27: March 16, 1859: "At home – A company of Pike's Peak emigrants Faurote, Crandall, Wilcox and others stopped at the grove and stayed all night – fine day – Brainard and Abe Rutt took the third degree of Masonry." *From Daniel M. Valentine's Diary, courtesy of Kansasmemory.org, Kansas State Historical Society.*

No doubt these funds were to be used on George's next adventure. In 1860, George, eighteen-year-old son Miles, and probably a company of men, left Iowa headed for Pike's Peak. Elvira and their son George W. very likely went as well, as there is no evidence that George ever again returned farther east than Omaha, Nebraska.

What must Lydia have thought was happening? Did she yet know of the mistress and child? Did she know George was never coming back? Did they say their good-byes, or did he simply abandon her in Winterset, Iowa allowing her to think that he was simply on one of his adventures? A family "rumor" was that George begged Lydia to go west with him, but she refused. He supposedly returned or wrote to her, begging, but she was adamant. I find this highly unlikely for reasons that will reveal themselves farther along in this book, but I will leave it to you, dear reader, to decide how believable you find that rumor to be.

One must also wonder what George's son Miles thought of it all. His father had just left his mother and family for a mistress and child. He did clearly forgive his father his indiscretions – he maintained contact with his father until George's death – seemingly the only child to have done so.

It doesn't appear that George or Miles were successful in finding gold at Pike's Peak. Perhaps they worked the mines for a time, but their next endeavor, presumably together, was running an Omaha to Denver ox team freight line. In Miles' obituary in the *Tulare Advance-Register* on December 14, 1916, it says that Miles "took part in a number of Indian fights along the Platte River." An article in the *Plattsmouth Journal* of March 12, 1903 mentions Miles having been seriously injured by an arrow through his right shoulder during an Indian attack on his employer's ranch in Julesburg, Colorado in 1865.

Denver was the "mecca" for many western freighters and served the western territories as a distributing point. Freighting was a challenging, dirty, exhausting and dangerous occupation.

They were a class that liked fun, enjoyed freedom, despised luxury, and took no note of danger or privation; and they were not of the dumb and stupid class of society. Many were educated, and some of them were gifted... Theirs was a rough life, a hard life, a dangerous life, and withal a romantic life. They fill a place in history that is due to those who dared to venture, who dared to risk, who dared to fight, who dared to die that by so doing they might ever guide, ever urge, and ever point an overland train prairie ward.

Floyd E. Breese

Elvira and George W. would have likely remained in or near Denver as George ran the freight train back and forth, which would have been no easy life for them, either.

In an 1884 writing by Augusta (Pierce) Tabor, she speaks of the challenges of being a woman in Colorado when she and her husband arrived in 1859. When they arrived in Denver, she was the eleventh woman to arrive there and perhaps only one of several white women. They relocated to Golden, Colorado and she was left in camp as her husband went into the mountains in search of gold. She said:

> *I stayed in camp and took care of the cattle and the provisions. We had six months of provisions with us. The cattle were foot-sore and could not go far but I kept them from straying. I stayed there quite alone; there was no one there, no Indians, nothing there but just myself and our teams, silence reigned around, not a soul but me and my baby, and I was a weakly woman, not nearly so strong as I am now.*

She was the first woman in Colorado City and California Gulch. She noted that there were "a good many Indians in the country in 1859 and 1860, but at that time they were friendly so we did not fear them." She gives us some insight into what a woman's life was like at the time. She said:

> *Really the women did more in the early days than the men. There was so much for them to do, the sick to take care of. I have had so many unfortunate men shot by accident, brought to my cabin to take care of. There were so many men who could not cook and did not like men's cooking and would insist upon boarding where there was a woman and they would board there all they could.*

Augusta became a very astute businesswoman and helped her husband become one of the wealthiest men in the United States. She was one of the wealthiest women in Denver at the time of her death in 1895. In 1991, she was inducted into the Colorado Women's Hall of Fame and the National Mining Hall of Fame.

Colorado wasn't devoid of females, however. In a diary kept by Dr. George M. Willing, he made an entry on May 25, 1859, saying:

In some of the trains there is quite a number of females. How they make out is a marvel to me. It is hard enough on a man. With one train, an American is returning to New Mexico, with his family consisting of wife and four grown daughters. On the road one of the daughters was brought to the bed of a baby, her husband having died only two days previously. I never witnessed such distress in my life, and pray I never may again.

George, Elvira and George W.'s time in Colorado was fairly short lived. Circa 1862, they moved on to Utah and then to Sacramento, California – in both places running hotels. They then disappear from official records until 1864, when they pop up in Arizona with a newborn baby girl.

Miles relocated to Nebraska City, Otoe County, Nebraska by 1868, though it was likely sooner. He may have still been involved in freighting to Denver for some time, as Nebraska City was a main starting point of several freight lines, the largest being that of Russell, Majors and Waddell. It was more of a freighting base than it was a town. It depended almost entirely for its support on the transportation of freight westward.

He married Frances J. "Fannie" Mann on January 16, 1868 in Otoe County, Nebraska. Their first three children were born in Nebraska, after which they moved to California.

Lydia was now a single, abandoned mother with six children, one of which was a newborn. Her eldest, Samuel, helped her to run the St. Nicholas Hotel. John Milton was seventeen and also helping with the St. Nicholas. Caroline, the eldest daughter, fourteen when her father left, surely had her hands full helping with the children and home chores. One can hardly imagine what it must have felt like to be deserted, much less just prior to the outbreak of war, with a houseful of young children. The strength it must have taken to carry on, to put one foot in front of the other, to tend to home and children, is inconceivable. She would have also carried the shame of abandonment, unfair as that would have been.

There is no reason to believe that Lydia – nor their children, with the exclusion of Miles - ever saw George again. As if times couldn't get much harder, not long after George left his family, the Civil War broke out. On January 1, 1862, George and Lydia's son John Milton enlisted. He was severely wounded in the leg at the Battle of Pea Ridge in Arkansas on March 7, 1862 and discharged.

In June 1863, their son Samuel appears on the Civil War draft registration as a hotelkeeper, but he did not go to war. On December 14, 1863, Samuel married Almyra Root in Cass County, Iowa. It was the first marriage of any of George's children, but he was not present. He would not be present for any of his children's weddings. Except for Miles' children, he would never know any of his future grandchildren.

Figure 28: This image may be the first ever taken of Denver City, Kansas Territory. The name was changed to Denver in 1902.

Larimer St. Denver City looking north east, 1858-1860 *by Rufus E. Cable. Courtesy of Denver Public Library, Western History Collection, [X-22056]*

Figure 29: Wagon train in Denver City, Kansas Territory, 1865.

David Bruce Powers' Train *of Fort Leavenworth at Denver by William G. Chamberlain. Collection of Fred M. Mazzulla. Amon Carter Museum of American Art, Fort Worth, Texas. Street Scene in Denver, 1865. Image in the public domain.*

CHAPTER 8
LA PAZ, ARIZONA

Once again, George found himself irresistibly drawn by the sparkle of gold, this time leading him to Arizona. Gold had been discovered near La Paz in 1862 by mountain man Pauline Weaver, triggering the Colorado River Gold Rush. The town began to grow soon afterward, although the placers were largely exhausted by 1863. Once again, George was just a little too late.

The westernmost confrontation of the Civil War occurred at La Paz on May 20, 1863. A man recently released from the detention center at Fort Yuma ambushed unarmed soldiers, killing one and leaving another mortally wounded. He escaped into the desert, where he died of exposure and dehydration.

By October 1863, George, Elvira and son George W. had made their way to Arizona Territory, where George was running a whiskey mill and boarding house in the gold boom town of La Paz.

La Paz, situated in the Sonoran Desert region, consisted of desert landscape characterized by sparse vegetation, sandy soils and various types of cacti. It was exceedingly hot in summer; the average high in July being 107 degrees Fahrenheit.

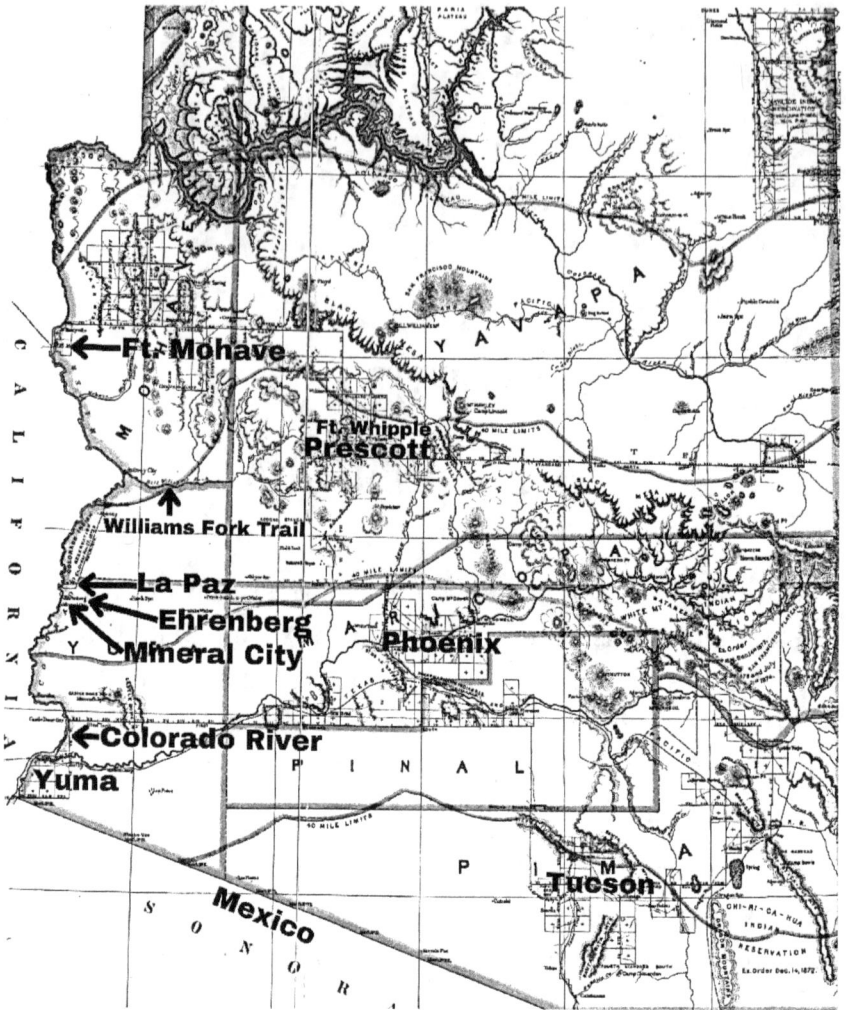

Figure 30: Arizona Territory 1876. United States Land Office, Washington, D.C. Text added for easier viewing.

La Paz was located 5.8 miles north of present-day Interstate 10 and just across the Colorado River from what is now Blythe, California. During the 1860s, it ranked with Tucson and Prescott as one of the most important communities in Arizona Territory. Born in the flurry of placer mining activity along the Colorado River, La Paz became the main departure point for more extensive prospecting in central Arizona. With a prime location on a navigable lagoon of the Colorado River, it evolved into a transfer point for freight brought via steamer from San Francisco destined for the interior, and for the return shipments of ore from the mines of central Arizona.

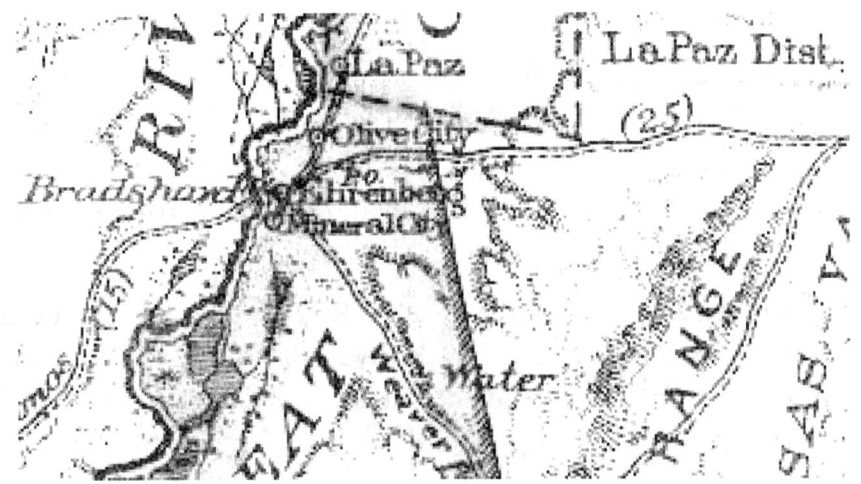

Figure 31: Close up of La Paz, Arizona area including Olive City, (old) Ehrenberg and Mineral City. The Bradshaw Trail comes in from the west. Official Map of The Territory of Arizona, The Graphic Co., New York by E.A. Eckhoff and P. Riecker, Civil Engineers, 1880.

As with any mining town, it had its share of outlaws and trouble. It had saloons, hotels, restaurants, a brewery, blacksmiths, bakeries and shops, but it had no schools or churches. It also had very few women in 1864; there were 250 American or European men, but only five Anglo women. Mexicans, on the other hand, came to La Paz in families, of which sixty-eight were women.

La Paz was the governmental seat of Yuma County, and as such filled a significant position in Arizona's territorial affairs. Perhaps most important, the town stood at the terminus of the main overland road from Los Angeles, and therefore acted as the western gateway for immigration to Arizona Territory.

WILLIAM D. BRADSHAW

William D. Bradshaw was a United States western pioneer and prospector. He is best remembered for forging the 180-mile-long Bradshaw Road, also known as the Road to La Paz and the Gold Road, in 1862 from San Bernardino, California to La Paz. Prior to then, getting to La Paz from California required going all the way south to Yuma and back up the river, which was a great deal longer. With news of gold in La Paz, prospectors needed a more direct route and Mr. Bradshaw and eight other men, with the help of the Cahuilla Indian tribe, succeeded in finding it.

Initially this gave the populated areas of California's west coast a more direct route to the Colorado River Gold Rush fields, but more importantly, the trail opened up the Southern California Colorado Desert region, and beyond, to settlement and development.

From 1862 to 1877, the Bradshaw Road was the main stagecoach and wagon route between Southern California and the gold fields of La Paz and other points west in Arizona. Olive City, first named "Olivia," six miles south of La Paz, was the first Bradshaw ferry crossing for the trail.

Olive City's namesake was Olive Ann Oatman (1837 – 1903), who was kidnapped with her sister Mary Ann by Indians in 1851 near Yuma, Arizona. Her parents and four siblings were killed, although her brother, Lorenzo Dow Oatman, was left for dead. She and her sister were enslaved and spent a year with the tribe before being traded to the Mohave Indians, where Olive spent the next four years. Her sister Mary Ann died while with the Mohave.

She was traded back to the Americans in 1856 for one horse, six pounds of beads and some fur blankets. When Olive returned, she was nineteen years old, had lost the ability to speak English, and bore an Indian tattoo on her chin.

Figure 32: Olive Oatman by Benjamin F. Powelson 1863. National Portrait Gallery, Smithsonian Institution, Washington, D.C. Image in the public domain.

In the fall of 1864, Mineral City and landing was established a mile down the river and Bradshaw's ferry was moved there, to the detriment of Olive City. It became the new Bradshaw ferry crossing. It consisted of a few tents, crude huts and sixteen men.

The Bradshaw Trail still exists today but only as a remnant of the Bradshaw Road. It is now just seventy miles in length.

Bradshaw died in Mineral City on December 2, 1864, after he slashed his own throat with a drawing knife. Newspaper reports at the time stated Bradshaw had committed suicide. Given the nature of his death and lack of witnesses, some historians believe he was murdered. The December 17, 1864 *Los Angeles Daily News* said, "Bradshaw had been on one of his "big benders" – was probably under the influence of liquor at the time; he was pursued by ghosts, etc.; he walked deliberately into a carpenter's shop, took up a drawing-knife, and with one stroke nearly severed his head from his shoulders." Bradshaw was a known alcoholic and some believe he may have been in withdrawal and seeing hallucinations. He was buried in the town cemetery at the "end of his road from San Bernardino."

The "end of his road" would have been at Mineral City, Arizona, which was two miles north of modern-day Ehrenberg, Arizona. All that exists of the original Ehrenberg is the Ehrenberg Pioneer Cemetery, where burials began about 1862. It has twenty-two memorials on the website Find A Grave, but there are likely a great many more. Many graves are covered with stones and most have no markers. A pioneer, Martha Summerhayes, wrote of the cemetery:

From (husband) Jack's diary: Aug. 23rd. Heat awful. Pringle died today. He was the third soldier to succumb. It seemed to me their fate was a hard one. To die, down in a wretched place, to be rolled in a blanket and buried on those desert shores, with nothing but a heap of stones to mark their graves.

The next day I asked Jack to walk to the grave-yard with me. He postponed it from day to day, but I insisted upon going. At last, he took me to see it.

There was no enclosure, but the bare, sloping, sandy place was sprinkled with graves, marked by heaps of stones, and in some instance by rude crosses of wood, some of which had been wrenched from their upright position by the fierce sand-storms. There was not a blade of grass, a tree, or a flower. I walked about among these graves, and close beside some of them I saw deep holes and whitened bones. I was quite ignorant or unthinking, and asked what the holes were.

"It is where the coyotes and wolves come in the nights," said Jack.

My heart sickened as I thought of these horrors, and I wonder if Ehrenburg held anything in store for me worse than what I had already seen. We turned away from this unhallowed grave-yard and walked to our quarters. I had never known much about "nerves," but I began to see specters in the nights, and those ghastly graves with their coyote-holes were ever before me. The place was but a stone's throw from us, and the uneasy spirits from these desecrated graves began to haunt me. I couldn't not sit alone on the porch at night, for they peered through the lattice, and mocked at me, and beckoned. Some had no heads, some no arms, but they pointed or nodded towards the gruesome burying-ground: "You'll be with us soon, you'll be with us soon."

Figure 33: Ehrenberg, Arizona Pioneer Cemetery, courtesy of Lois Ann Preston, American Pioneer and Cemetery Research Project: https://www.apcrp.org/

At one time the cemetery may have been known as "Boot Hill Cemetery." Author Lambert Florin said in 1967, "From Blythe, California, go east across Colorado River into Arizona. Just after crossing note gravel exiting left (north), this is the location of Ehrenberg . . . Almost at intersection is Boot Hill Cemetery, one of (the) bleakest, most forlorn in West. Piles of stone mark graves, identification totally lacking. Some markers come tantalizingly close to being legible. Imposing monument erected by highway crews is desecrated by vandals. Careful search east of exit road reveals some scanty adobe ruins."

George and Elvira had another child together circa April 1864; a daughter named Arizona. Her entry in the Arizona United States Territorial Census in 1864 is the one record that exists to show that she ever lived. It is not known when or where she died, nor where she was buried.

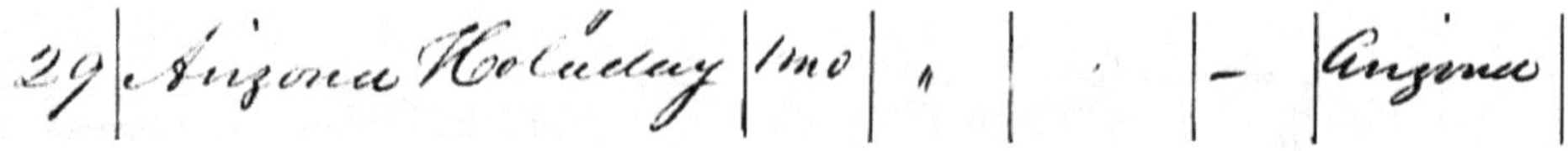

Figure 34: Arizona Holaday on the Arizona United States Territorial Census record, May 1864. The record lists her as one month old and born in Arizona (Territory). Along with her, George, Elvira and George W. are also listed.

Elvira died in La Paz on July 5, 1864. A simple blurb in the *Arizona Miner* stated that she died in La Paz at age thirty-five, with no further details. It is not known where Elvira was buried and if she and her daughter both found their final resting places under piles of stones. George now had a five-year-old son and possibly an infant daughter to take care of by himself.

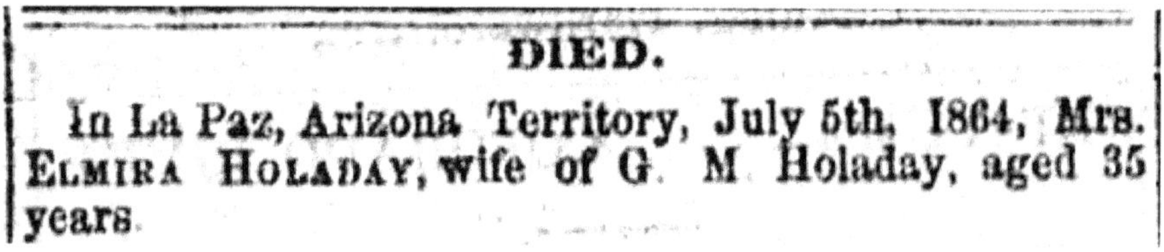

DIED.

In La Paz, Arizona Territory, July 5th, 1864, Mrs. ELMIRA HOLADAY, wife of G. M. Holaday, aged 35 years.

Figure 35: The Arizona Miner August 10, 1864. Chronicling America: Historic American Newspapers. Library of Congress.

APACHES

As the eastern half of the United States was occupied with the Civil War, men in the mining camps were quite content to pan gold and ignore it. After the Civil War, nearly all troops were withdrawn from Arizona and as a result, Indian attacks on white settlers and their property increased.

Most mining camps of Arizona Territory were dependent on

freighters to bring in supplies from the river landing at La Paz. Until the establishment of a military post at La Paz, the Indians had been waylaying these shipments with a heavy toll of life and supplies. If a supply train was too big to safety annihilate, the Indians would bargain, taking one of the wagons in exchange for safe passage. It was suicide for a freighter to take to the trail alone. The army even tried to out-maneuver the Indians by hiring their leaders as scouts or guides, but the plunderings and massacres continued.

There was no tribe more despised by the settlers than the Apache. In Patrick Hamilton's 1883 *The Resources of Arizona,* his intense feelings of anger, hatred, bitterness, and frustration toward the Apache were expressed with powerful and vivid language.[11]

In regard to the Apache, Mr. Hamilton said:

They are capable of standing much fatigue and hardship and can make long journeys over the barren plains and mountains without food or drink. They are thieves by nature and murderers by instinct. In their wild state they had no fixed habitation, and roamed through the mountains, improvising a rude shelter for a few days where game or mescal was abundant. Yet this handful of savages have virtually maintained a reign of terror in Arizona and northern Mexico until within the last few years. They are adept at savage warfare and are masters of every stratagem to entrap the unwary traveler. Never giving battle on the open plain, they always lay hidden behind some rock or bush and surprised their victim when he least expected an attack.

---

[11] Patrick Hamilton (1843 – 1888) came from Ireland to the United States at age thirteen. In 1873, he was commissioned by the legislature to prepare a publication on the resources of Arizona for distribution in the east. He was elected a member of the legislature for Yavapai County, Arizona in 1878. He died of tuberculosis.

Of all Indians, the Apache seems less disposed to adopt the habits and mode of life of the white man. He is a savage, pure and simple, and can no more be tamed than a tiger or a wildcat.

Figure 36: Apache Indians. Geronimo (1829 – 1909) at far right. From 1850 to 1886, Geronimo joined with the members of three other central Apache bands to carry out numerous raids, as well as fight against Mexican and U.S. military campaigns in Mexico, New Mexico and Arizona. Image by C.S. Fly, 1886. Image in the public domain.

He also offered sharp criticism concerning the Apache at the San Carlos, Arizona reservation, and the reservation system in general:

The reservation system has been tried and proved a failure. It has become a breeding-place for assassins, an asylum for murderers and marauders, a home for thieves and outlaws, a shelter for the most bloodthirsty villains that ever cumbered the earth. For years the government has expended money with a lavish hand in maintaining these wretches in idleness and ease. Abundance of food and clothing, and the best medical care have been theirs. Living in one of the finest farming regions in the Territory, and provided with the latest improved and costliest of farming machinery, no effort has been made to compel these lazy vagabonds to till the soil and make themselves self-sustaining.

The people are taxed to support a horde of banditti who learn nothing but the vices which spring from idleness and sloth. Into the hands of these untamed thugs the government has placed arms and ammunition. Whenever life on the reservation becomes too monotonous, they hie themselves forth, killing and destroying everything in their path. When hard-pressed they cross the border into Mexico, and there indulge in the same deviltry. When they tire of this pastime, and rations run short, they steal back to the San Carlos, there to rest and feast until they get ready for another raid. This is the way the reservation system has worked in Arizona, and is it any wonder the people have become exasperated, and that many of them demand total extermination as the only solution of the Indian problem.

The people of Arizona demand a radical change. They believe the presence of so large a body of Apaches almost in the heart of the Territory, is a constant menace to its peace, and a steady drawback to its material advancement. They know that some of the finest grazing and farming, and the richest mineral lands are closed to occupation and settlement on account of the presence of these worthless savages. They also know that a large portion of the public domain has been set apart for the exclusive use of Indians, and believe thither they should be sent. There is abundance of room in the Indian Territory and there let the Apaches go. Let them be made to work and learn to become self-sustaining. This is the true solution of the Arizona Indian problem, and the one which will meet the approbation of every citizen who has the interests of the Territory at heart. A few thousand savages, whose worthless lives, all combined are not worth that of one honest white man, have too long retarded the advancement of one of the richest regions of the West, too long have obstructed the path of progress, and cast a shadow on the Territory's prosperity.

The Apache must go. The land he has so long cursed with his presence will rejoice when the last of his race shall have passed beyond her borders.

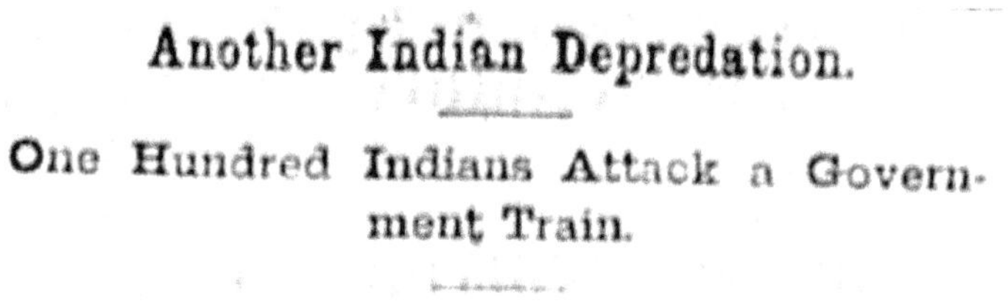

Another Indian Depredation.

One Hundred Indians Attack a Government Train.

Figure 37: Weekly Journal Miner, *June 26, 1869. Chronicling America: Historic American Newspapers. Library of Congress.*

His vitriol was uniquely directed toward the Apache, with no other group bearing the same level of contempt. He said:

… The people find no particular objection to any but the Apache tribe. The other Indians are peaceable and well-disposed, and inclined to earn a livelihood by their own exertions. While it is true that the Reservation set apart for the Pimas and Maricopas contains some of the finest farming lands in the Territory, and is much larger than they will ever bring under cultivation, still their white neighbors do not complain at their petty pilfering, and the trouble and

annoyance which they often cause to settlers. But for the Apache they have no room. For long years they have suffered at his hands and seen some of their best and bravest offered as a sacrifice to his insatiable hate. His history is written in blood, and his presence is a continual menace to the peace, and an obstacle in the path of the country's every interest. He occupies one of the most desirable regions in the entire Territory, and prevents the coming of immigration and the investment of capital. Let him be removed and his power for mischief will be at an end.

King S. Woolsey, a leader, politician, explorer and pioneer, enjoyed a wide reputation in Arizona Territory during the 1860s as an Indian fighter. He shared the same hatred of the Apaches. A handsome, energetic man, he gained much of his fame in 1864 by leading three expeditions of volunteer militia into the Tonto and Pinal Mountains in search of Apaches who had stolen horses from miners and ranchers near Prescott.

On May 1, 1864 in La Paz, a meeting convened at the City Hotel, where George called the assembly to order. A statement made on April 19, 1864 by the Hon. Robert C. McCormick, Secretary of the Territory, was read aloud. In effect, it was a statement of support for another expedition to be led by Woolsey against the Pinal Apache Indians.

Woolsey wanted to secure supplies and volunteers for the upcoming expedition. Seventy men had already volunteered. A number of contributions were made of money, flour, coffee, sugar, bacon, beans and miscellaneous goods. George pledged $10 – the 2023 equivalent of about $200. Woolsey said that the objective of the expedition was to take in Tonto Chief "Big Rump," and then push on further east, prospecting the country as far as their provisions would allow.

On June 1, 1864, ninety-three men set out into the Apache domain along the Verde River. The men spent most of their time prospecting and exploring when unable to find any Indians to fight. Each time they located an encampment, it had been hastily abandoned and all former inhabitants gone.

There was but one incident on this expedition, the death of John W. Beauchamp. He had left camp to go to the top of a mountain where the expedition was camping. Upon arriving near the top, he was waylaid by six Indians who shot, lanced, stripped him, and left him for dead. Of course, this only infuriated the expedition, super igniting their hatred. An article in the *Arizona Miner* said, "His (Beauchamp's) brutal butchery by the savages adds another to our many reasons for hastening their extermination. The men who were with Woolsey, and all who knew Beauchamp will eagerly avenge his death."

The expedition was turned over to Major Joseph Smith, but he found it impossible to continue due to lack of provisions and heavy rains. At that point the expedition was abandoned. Woolsey returned home eighty-seven days after the expedition started.

FIRST ARIZONA TERRITORIAL LEGISLATURE

The Arizona Territorial Legislature was the legislative body of Arizona Territory. It consisted of a lower house, the House of Representatives, and an upper house, the Council. Woolsey was elected to represent the third district in the Council.

In an election held at George's home in La Paz on July 18, 1864, he was elected to represent La Paz in the House of Representatives.

In late July 1864, George, along with a Mr. Brown and a Mr. C. Davidson, traveled the 170-mile-long Williams Fork Trail from La Paz to Prescott. The weather was scorching hot and about a mile outside of Prescott, Mr. Davidson succumbed to heatstroke and could not continue. George and Mr. Brown pressed on to Prescott to find help, leaving Davidson on the trail. Several men hurried back with water and supplies, but it was too late and Davidson had died.

On August 24, the *Arizona Miner* reported that George was "still there" (in Prescott) and that he seemed to like Prescott "exceedingly." September 29, 1864 was the first session of the Territorial Assembly in Prescott. In October, George was made the temporary speaker of the House of Representatives and deputy postmaster.

George introduced two bills in his time in the Territorial Legislature. The first was to allow William D. Bradshaw and his associates to construct, maintain and keep a ferry across the Colorado River from La Paz to Mineral City, Arizona, with exclusive rights for twenty years. It was approved November 7, 1864.

Meanwhile in Iowa... *On November 8, 1864, George and Lydia's eldest daughter Caroline married Benjamin Franklin Murray in Winterset, Iowa.*

The next was to provide for the payment of certain expenses incurred in the late Indian campaign under King Woolsey. The bill called for it to be the duty of the Board of Auditors to audit the claims submitted by Woolsey regarding the campaign against the Apache Indians. The total sum was not to exceed $1,484 – the 2023 equivalent of about $28K. The bill was approved November 9, 1864.

An attempt, likely supported by George, was made to move the territorial capital to La Paz, but those efforts were defeated.

While many mining settlements fade with the depletion of resources and market fluctuations, La Paz met a premature end not by economic forces, but rather by the unpredictable whims of the river. During the high-water season of 1866, the Colorado River flooded and cut a new channel. It left La Paz landlocked, two miles from the nearest convenient steamer boat landing. A town situated by a river, yet lacking both the river and its landing, is destined for hardship and failure. Most soon packed up and moved south to Mineral City. La Paz was nearly abandoned by 1871 and a ghost town by 1875. The county seat was moved to Yuma.

HUALAPAI

About one hundred miles to the north of La Paz, around Mohave City, Arizona (now a ghost town), friction between prospectors and the local Hualapai Indians had been growing and eventually erupted into warfare. When the whites started building the Santa Fe Railroad for mining purposes, they demanded that the Hualapai vacate their homes. The Hualapai resisted and began raids on the toll road from Mohave City to Prescott, Arizona. A treaty was negotiated but was soon broken with the murder of Hualapai sub tribal Chief Wauba Yuba and his two sons by a white teamster from Prescott. They had been on a goodwill mission to negotiate with the whites when they were murdered. After the murders, raids by the Hualapai began in full force on mining camps and settlers. This sparked the Hualapai Wars.

The cavalry responded with the assistance of the Mohave Indians, enemies of the Hualapai, by attacking Hualapai rancherias and razing them. The Battle of Cherum Peak, in January 1868, broke the resistance of the Hualapai as whooping cough and dysentery further weakened their ranks. The Hualapai surrendered in 1869 and they were forcibly relocated to a camp near Parker, Arizona.

In 1874, the Hualapai, the "People of the Tall Pines," were cruelly marched against their will to La Paz. Many died in the two-week, 160-mile journey. General George Crook noted that the Hualapai, mountain Indians, suffered terribly in the sweltering heat and desert conditions of the Lower Colorado River. Many of those who managed to survive the trip later died of starvation and disease.

Kathad Ganavj related his grandmother's experience as a young girl forced to make the grueling march to La Paz in the book, *Coyote Stories*. The excerpt may be found at: https://hualapai-nsn.gov/wp-content/uploads/2015/03/KathadGanavjlapazstory.pdf. She and her grandfather both made the march, with she helping and leading him. He died after being whipped for not being able to walk any further.

It is a deeply disturbing account of both young and old being forced to march naked at gunpoint, surrounded by soldiers on horseback and beaten and whipped if they did not move quickly enough. Those who became ill or were injured were left to die on the trail. They were dependent on what little food they brought with them and were not fed.

They arrived in La Paz in late spring, and it was already intensely hot. There was no protection or shelter from the sun. The rations they were given were often rancid and spoiled, which led to illness and death. As they died, they were buried in the ditches, sand and washes. No exact numbers can be quoted, but some estimate that perhaps one third or more of the Hualapai died either on the march or in the inhumane conditions at La Paz.

A year after their arrival, the Hualapai escaped. Many returned to their lands in northwestern Arizona. They were not pursued, and were spared further military action, but once they returned home, they found that white men occupied their homelands.

Mr. Hamilton spoke far more fondly of the Hualapai. He also again made his disdain for the government reservation system policy clear when he said:

The Hualapai tribe are an offshoot of the Apache nation, and, in appearance, much resemble the latter. They live in the barren mountain regions of Mohave County, eking out a precarious existence on roots, lizards, rats, mesquite beans, mescal, and the little wild game which the country affords. They also hang around the different mining camps, doing odd jobs and picking up any crumb which may fall from the table of the miner or prospector. They were at one time on the Colorado reservation, but the enervating climate of the river bottoms was fatal to Indians born and bred in the pure, bracing air of the mountains, and they returned to their native hills. The Hualapais are a brave and warlike race, and caused the early settlers of northern Arizona much trouble. They number about 800, with a head chief, and many small bands ruled by captains.

They did good service against the hostile Apaches, many of them enlisting as scouts and fighting bravely by the side of the troops. They are experts in the use of the rifle, and long intercourse with the whites has taught them all the vices of the paleface. These Indians have been several times on the brink of starvation, and have to depend nearly altogether on the bounty of the settlers. Although they 'have done the State some service,' and earned the gratitude of the people by their services against the common enemy, they are neglected by the government, and allowed to gain a subsistence as best they may. But it does not seem to be the policy of the Indian department to reward or encourage peaceful tribes. Flour, beef, coffee, sugar, clothing and other good things are only given to those "gentle savages" who can point with pride to the white scalps which adorn their teepees on the San Carlos. But such is our Indian policy.

Today, the Hualapai live on a reservation that encompasses a million acres along 108 miles of the Colorado River and the Grand Canyon. Their tribal capital is at Peach Springs, Arizona. Each year the tribe holds the Hualapai La Paz Trail of Tears Run to commemorate the survivors for their perseverance.

A 1912 flood melted all the adobe structures of La Paz, turning them into dirt mounds. Remnants of some old stone foundations have been partially excavated and can be seen today near the Hualapai Monument. The monument is six miles north of present-day Ehrenberg, Arizona.

La Paz was once a place of great prosperity, having at its height, a population of perhaps thousands. It was of immense importance all through the Civil War and only missed being named the capital city of Arizona Territory by one vote. It was the county seat of Yuma County until 1870.

It was also a place of profound sorrow and despair, witnessing deprivation, desperation, death, misery and starvation. When gold miners failed to find success, they moved on to more promising prospects. However, for the Hualapai, survival itself was a fortunate outcome.

Figure 38: The ruins of La Paz about 1890. Image in the public domain.

Figure 39: An old foundation in the ruins of La Paz. Image courtesy of Nesta Skychild.

Figure 40: The Hualapai Monument. Image courtesy of Nesta Skychild.

The words on the Hualapai monument read:

In Memory of Hualapai Ancestors

Yu' Nyihay Jamj Vo:jo

— La Paz Trail of Tears - April 21, 1874 – April 21, 1875 —

We honor our ancestors who died violent deaths at the hands of their captors and at this concentration camp. We greet the spirits of our ancestors and embrace their strength and above all else, their will to survive this holocaust. The Hualapai People's strength and cultural survival endures to all future generations to come.

CHAPTER 9
PRESCOTT, ARIZONA

Prescott, Arizona was founded in May 1864 after gold was discovered in the Bradshaw Mountains, just south and east of present-day Prescott. It became the territorial capital of Arizona in 1864 and the county seat of newly created Yavapai County.

Once George went to Prescott in late July 1864, it doesn't appear that he returned to La Paz to live. In December 1864, the *Los Angeles Daily News* of December 17, 1864 said "The Hon. G.M. Holliday, member of the Arizona Legislature, from the La Paz District, gave us a call on yesterday; having arrived here a day or two since, direct from the Capital." (It is assumed "the Capital" being referred to is Sacramento.)

Thus far, almost nothing can be found of his activities from January 1865 to January 1866.

Adventurers seeking opportunities came from far and wide. Miners were in search of gold; farmers and ranchers were seeking land to make new beginnings. As a young western frontier town, it saw its share of gunslingers, shootouts and overall rowdy behavior.

Its growth came at the expense of the Yavapai Indians, the

natives who had occupied the region for centuries before the influx of those drawn there by the promise of riches and opportunity. They were forced onto reservations at Camp Verde and then to San Carlos Apache Reservation. Their forced walk from Camp Verde to San Carlos was 180 miles over snow covered mountains and rivers. It is estimated that 115 Yavapai and Apaches died along the way. They were not allowed to perform traditional burial ceremonies and had to leave the bodies of loved ones behind in the snow.

The first sale of lots in Prescott was auctioned off on June 4, 1864 and the erection of buildings began immediately. By late July, Prescott would boast the office of the newspaper the *Arizona Miner*, a billiard saloon, a doctor's office, store, a hotel, a restaurant and bar called the Juniper House built, or nearly so.

Figure 41: An early photograph of Prescott, Arizona, 1864. In the center is the Arizona Brewery. Of the people in the center of the photograph, one appears to be a young boy. Photograph of the Arizona Territorial capitol in Prescott (Ariz.), shortly after its construction. Used with permission. Credit: Arizona State Library, Archives and Public Records, History and Archives Division, Phoenix, #96-9438

The Juniper House offered dinner of mutton broth, bean soup, beef soup, beef potpie, venison potpie, apple roll with sauce and other choices for the July 4, 1864 celebratory meal. Soon after, a school was built, along with a lumber mill, brickyard, more stores, hotels, farms and ranches. It was the dominant political center of the territory and was protected and influenced by the presence of the army post of Fort Whipple, which was established in May 1864 one and a half miles away. It was a large rectangular pine log stockade.

Prescott remained the territorial capital until 1867, when it was moved to Tucson. It was eventually moved back to Prescott, and then to Phoenix, Arizona, where it remains.

WHISKEY ROW

The original Whiskey Row in Prescott was comprised of the one hundred block of Montezuma Street and portions of the adjacent Cortez and Granite Streets. Catering to the cowboys, miners, gamblers and outlaws, there was no shortage of drinking establishments, gambling halls, poker parlors, restaurants and brothels. At one point, forty saloons were crowded into the area. The saloons were street level, while the brothels were located above.

THE MONTEZUMA SALOON

George pops up again in January 1866, living in a "little room" on Granite Street, when he opened the Montezuma Saloon at 108 (South) Montezuma Street on lot seventeen. His core offerings were fine California wines, and his bartender was a man by the name of Andrew "Jack" Shanks.

The *Arizona Miner* published the following on January 24, 1866, "Holaday has left his little room on Granite Street, and taken the bar at the Montezuma. We (illegible) that in addition to the fine stock of liquors he recently received from Campbell, who is going inside. Holaday undoubtedly has the genuine articles, and Shanks, his barkeeper, knows how to deal it out."

It is not known where little George W., about five and a half years old by now, nor his sister Arizona, if she was still alive, were at this time.

Not long after opening his saloon, on February 4, 1866, some belligerent, drunken soldiers from Fort Whipple were involved in a "lively row" in the Montezuma. A man was wounded in the wrist by gunfire and the furniture was smashed up. George abandoned the saloon the next day and went to San Francisco, California.

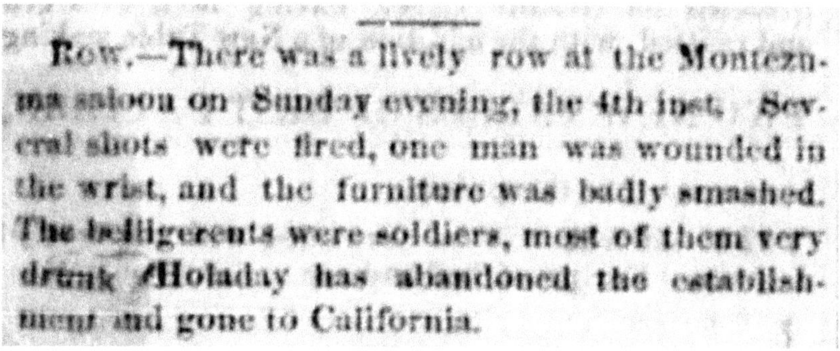

> Row.—There was a lively row at the Montezuma saloon on Sunday evening, the 4th inst. Several shots were fired, one man was wounded in the wrist, and the furniture was badly smashed. The belligerents were soldiers, most of them very drunk. Holaday has abandoned the establishment and gone to California.

Figure 42: Arizona Miner, February 14, 1866. Chronicling America: Historic American Newspapers. Library of Congress.

Meanwhile, in Iowa... *George and Lydia's first grandchild was born in Winterset, Iowa. Gertude Holaday was born on May 6, 1866, the daughter of their first-born son Samuel and wife Almyra (Root) Holaday.*

On June 22, 1866, while in San Francisco, George wrote a letter to the *Arizona Miner,* saying that he was going to be headed back to Prescott. He said, "Arizona now stands as well in the minds of the people as any mineral country in the Union, and I am confident that so soon as the Indian rumors cease there will be a large emigration to the Territory from California."

THE PINE TREE SALOON

George returned to Prescott, arriving on August 9, 1866. Soon after, he opened the Pine Tree Saloon at 160 (South) Montezuma Street, three doors north of Goodwin St., on lot thirty-five, where the original Prescott Post Office had been. It was attached to a twenty-four-hour bakery and coffee shop. It adjoined a new theatre owned by Mr. John Littig and Mr. McGinley.

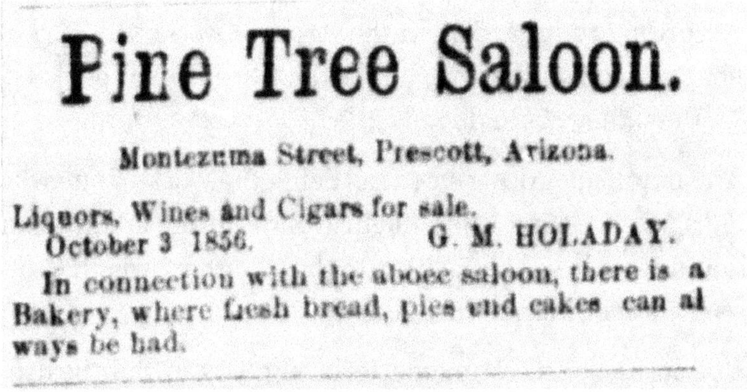

> **Pine Tree Saloon.**
>
> Montezuma Street, Prescott, Arizona.
>
> Liquors, Wines and Cigars for sale.
> October 3 1856.   G. M. HOLADAY.
>
> In connection with the aboee saloon, there is a Bakery, where fresh bread, pies and cakes can always be had.

Figure 43: Pine Tree Saloon Ad. Arizona Miner, October 27, 1866. Chronicling America: Historic American Newspapers. Library of Congress.

The property was just across from the Prescott town square. At the time, the only permanent structure in the square was a flagpole, which stood 144 feet tall.

In March of 1867, squatters, men who were mostly strangers to the area, arrived in Prescott and proceeded to stake and fence the town square. They were appropriating the lots for their own private use and selling them for exorbitant amounts. This was certainly not welcome by the residents and land owners of Prescott. Warnings to the squatters were printed in the *Arizona Miner* newspaper with a list of all those in opposition to the squatters. George's name was on the list, as was that of Mr. John Littig. The battle played out for some months, but was eventually settled against the squatters. It is with a touch of irony that George now found himself on the opposite side of squatters.

At 3:00 AM on May 2, 1867, in what the *Weekly Alta California* called the "first fire of consequence" in Prescott, the Pine Tree Saloon and the adjoining theatre burned to the ground. The bakery and a store owned by Governor McCormick were saved, although heavily damaged. The *Arizona Miner* newspaper office, located at the rear of the building, was severely scorched, but was also saved.

According to an article in the *Arizona Miner* on May 4, 1867, citizens "worked with a will, but in the (illegible) of buckets, hooks and ladders, they could do but little."

The newspaper described it as being the work of one who had a grudge against George. One might wonder if the arson was related to his and Mr. Littig's opposition to the squatters, who had been just across the street from their building.

The losses were estimated to be $3,000 to the theatre (2023 equivalent of $58K), $1,200 for George (2023 equivalent of $23K), $200 for McCormick's store (2023 equivalent of $4K), and $300 for Shroder's bakery (2023 equivalent of $6K).

This was apparently quite enough for George, and he left Arizona soon after to return to California. A July 4, 1883 fire burned most of Montezuma Street. The town was rebuilt, but mostly in wooden structures again and a second fire on July 14, 1900 nearly destroyed the entire business district. When rebuilding commenced the next time, it was all in brick and stone.

Today, the Birdcage Saloon in Prescott bears the address of 160 South Montezuma St., although the original location of the Pine Tree Saloon was on the corner.

CHAPTER 10
CALIFORNIA

Upon George's return to California in May 1867, he kept a bar and hotel in Petaluma, about thirty miles north of San Francisco, for about six months. His son George W. was eight years old by this time, and if Arizona was still alive, she was three. It is hard to imagine how George had parented during his saloon endeavors. What he needed now, though, was a wife and he soon found one.

In 1868, date unknown, George married Mary E. (Robinson) Finley in San Francisco, California. His new wife had five of her six biological children living with her, so George became a stepfather. Her youngest child, just two years old in 1868, was also named George Washington. As of the time of this writing, no marriage records have been located.

Meanwhile, in Nebraska... *On January 16, 1868, George and Lydia's son Miles married Frances J. "Fannie" Mann in Otoe County, Nebraska.*

California

Figure 44: Los Angeles Area Map 1880. H.J. Stevenson, U.S. Dept. Surveyor. Oakland, CA: C.L. Smith & Co., lith., 1880. Annotations added.

MARY E. ROBINSON FINLEY

Mary, born about 1833 in Tennessee, was the daughter of Irwin and Rhoda (Strong) Robinson. The family emigrated to California about 1853. Mary had first been married to James W. Finley and they had six biological children together. James had been married before and brought his two biological children to their marriage. It is not known if they divorced or if James died, but when Mary married George, she had five of her six biological children at home. Her oldest son, Samuel, had moved out of the home to live with his grandfather, Irwin Robinson.

Her second born, a daughter named Nancy Jane – "Nannie" - had married at just age thirteen, a year after her mother's 1868 marriage to George. The other children were Amanda Ellen, Derilda Adeline, James Thomas and George Washington Finley. (Not to be confused with George Washington Holaday).

Nancy Jane had eight children with her first husband George Washington Brians (yes, another George Washington!) before he died in 1890. She remarried in 1894 to Benjamin Franklin Vaughan in Morrow, Oregon. In 1903, she and Benjamin were killed in the Heppner, Oregon flood, which killed 247 people. It was a major flash flood that destroyed a large portion of Heppner and remains the deadliest natural disaster in Oregon and the second deadliest flash flood in the United States.

From the *Weekly Oregon Statesman* on June 26, 1903, entitled, "Love's Last Embrace:"

> *Five minutes before the flood struck the house of Dr. Vaughn he and wife were sitting in a hammock in their front yard talking with a neighbor, whose house was but fifteen feet away. When it began to rain they went inside and were never seen again until found, Tuesday morning, in a drift in*

the lower part of town, each locked firmly in the arms of the other. No vestige of their house has ever been found, and where it stood there is no mark whatever of a human habitation, save a few of the foundation stones, and the small cellar half filled with mud.

After their marriage, George and Mary moved to Southern California, where they initially rented a tract of land to farm. They lived in Spadra, San Jose Township, Los Angeles County, from about 1868 to 1870. On the 1870 United States Federal Census, George and Mary are listed in Spadra, along with George W. and George's stepchildren. Arizona does not appear, so it must be assumed that she has died or George allowed someone else to raise her. It is profoundly sad that there is no record of what happened to little Arizona Holaday. The stepchildren are listed with George's surname, albeit spelled incorrectly as "Holliday." There were 103 total dwellings.

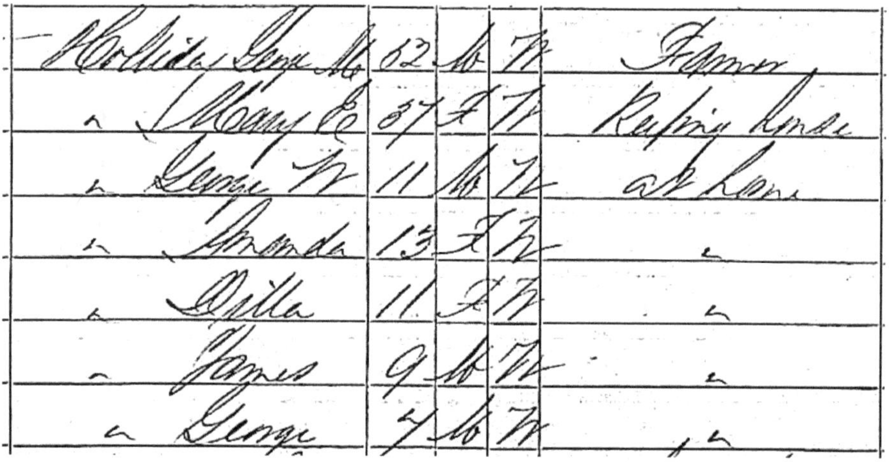

Holliday Geo M	62	M	W	Farmer
" Mary E	37	F	W	Keeping house
" George W	11	M	W	at home
" Amanda	13	F	W	"
" Willa	11	F	W	"
" James	9	M	W	"
" George	4	M	W	"

Figure 45: 1870 United States Federal Census, Los Angeles County, San Jose Township, Spadra, California

Meanwhile, in Iowa... *on February 6, 1868, George and Lydia's daughter Emma married Royal Oran Brown in Adair, Iowa.*

San Jose Township was a township in Los Angeles County that existed prior to the abolition of townships in California. It appeared as a subdivision of Los Angeles County in the 1860, 1870, and 1880 United States Federal Censuses. Spadra was a village within the township, officially founded in 1866. All that remains of it now are the Phillips Mansion and the Spadra Cemetery. Spadra was annexed into Pomona in the 1960s.

Meanwhile, in Iowa or Nebraska... *about 1871, George and Lydia's son John Milton married Mary Kinman.*

George was, as usual, a busy man in Southern California. He was on the move, as usual, in search of land to buy and new opportunities. In his travels, he apparently lost his black duster coat and a small blank pocket book containing receipts and papers. He placed an ad in the *Anaheim Gazette* in order to try to get them back.

Figure 46: The Anaheim Gazette, *September 16, 1871. Courtesy of Newspapers.com.*

In 1872, George bought a ranch in Rancho Las Bolsas Tract, located within present day Orange County, California. It was about forty miles south of Spadra and about six miles southwest of modern-day Anaheim. He engaged in farming.

Meanwhile, In Iowa... On July 16, 1873, George and Lydia's son William married Jennett Anna Gaylord in Montgomery County, Iowa.

Around 1876, they purchased another ranch in Westminster Colony, a part of Las Bolsas, just to the north.

Westminster Colony was founded by Rev. Lemuel Webber in 1870 as a Presbyterian temperance colony. "Las Bolsas" means "the pockets" and refers to pockets of land amongst the marsh wetlands of the Santa Ana River estuary. The ranch lands include the present-day cities of Huntington Beach, Garden Grove, Fountain Valley and Westminster, California. The name of Fountain Valley refers to the very high-water table in the area at the time the name was chosen, and the thirty-one flowing artesian wells in the area. George and the other early settlers constructed drainage canals to make the land usable for agriculture, which remained the dominant use of the land until the 1960s, when construction of large housing tracts accelerated.

Meanwhile, In Iowa... On June 19, 1877, George and Lydia's daughter Pauline married Albert Rush Dabney in Winterset, Iowa.

In April 1877, George was appointed Fountain Valley Township Justice of the Peace. Fountain Valley was just south of Westminster and Las Bolsas. On April 9, 1878, he was made a notary public for Fountain Valley, Los Angeles County, and again in 1880.

He resigned as justice of the peace in July 1880 and later in the summer or early fall set out for Tucson, Arizona. George, Mary, some family members and others made the six-hundred-mile trek to Tucson in thirty-one days. He took considerable livestock with them and was considering taking up residence there.

Apparently, Tucson wasn't to their liking and they returned to California by 1881. Mary bought forty acres of land in Wilmington Tract, Los Cerritos Rancho, Los Angeles County, paying $900 – the 2023 equivalent of about $27,000.

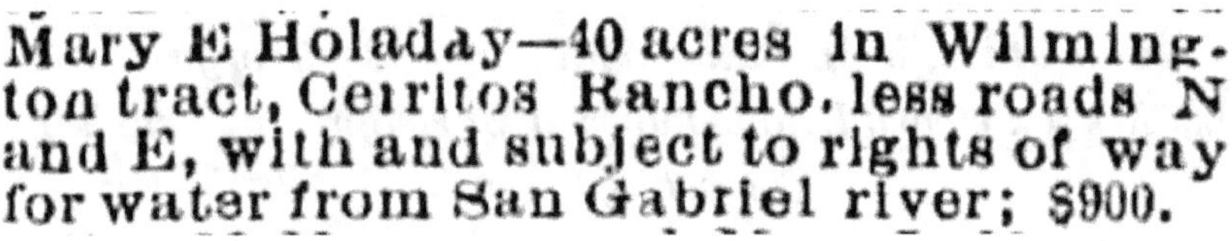

> Mary E Holaday—40 acres in Wilmington tract, Ceiritos Rancho, less roads N and E, with and subject to rights of way for water from San Gabriel river; $900.

Figure 47: Los Angeles Herald, *December 18, 1881. Courtesy of Newspapers.com.*

In 1882, George appears on the voter registration as living in Fountain Valley Township, Los Angeles, California.

Meanwhile, in Texas... *On February 10, 1882, George and Lydia's daughter Ellen married John Gallagher in Sherman, Texas.*

On November 4, 1883, Mary's son James Thomas Finley was married to Miss Lelia F. Owen in Los Cerritos. George and Mary were present for the ceremony.

The Republican County Convention was held on July 17, 1884 at Armory Hall to choose sixteen delegates to the State Republican Convention, that would be held in Sacramento about a week later.

Their responsibility was to nominate eight presidential electors and eight alternates - one from each congressional district and two at large from the entire state. They were also tasked with scheduling the time and place for the Sixth District Congressional Convention.

George, with three other men, was chosen as a delegate for Los Angeles City, Wilmington Township. George nominated Col. Henry H. Markham, the "dashing colonel from Pasadena," candidate for Congress from the Sixth District. Col. Markham represented California's sixth congressional district during the 49th United States Congress from 1885 to 1887. He went on to become the eighteenth governor of California, from 1891 to 1895.

Meanwhile, in Iowa... On May 10, 1885, George and Lydia's son Henry Delano married Mary Spies in Franklin Township, Iowa.

George and Mary remained at Los Cerritos until about September 1886, when they moved to San Fernando and George was appointed a justice of the peace.

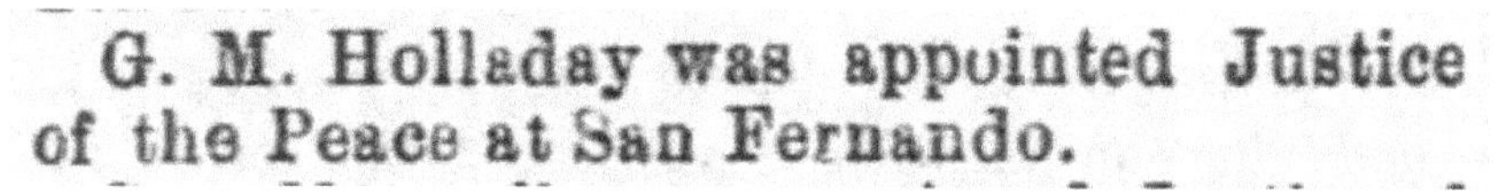

> G. M. Holladay was appointed Justice of the Peace at San Fernando.

Figure 48: The Los Angeles Times, *September 11, 1886. Courtesy of the California Digital Newspaper Collection, Center for Bibliographic Studies and Research, University of California, Riverside, http://cdnc.ucr.edu.*

They sold their Wilmington Tract land in 1887 to Jesse C. Thompson for $4,000. They purchased land from Mary S. Hadley in April 1888 for $4,000 – the 2023 equivalent of $128,000. Just months later, in October, in another transaction with Mary S. Hadley, they sold land to her for $2,700 – the 2023 equivalent of about $87,000. There were quite a few more land transactions not documented here. You could accurately say that George never lost his interest in buying and selling land.

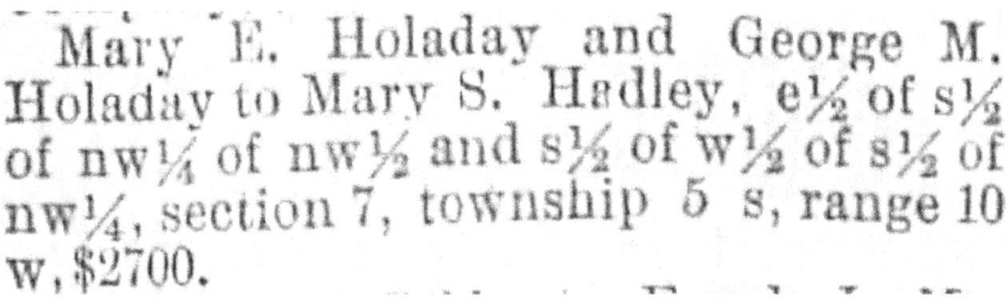

> Mary E. Holaday and George M. Holaday to Mary S. Hadley, e½ of s½ of nw¼ of nw½ and s½ of w½ of s½ of nw¼, section 7, township 5 s, range 10 w, $2700.

Figure 49: The Los Angeles Evening Express, *October 5, 1888. Courtesy of Newspapers.com.*

THE STACK MURDER

On Election Day, November 7, 1888, a very drunk and quarrelsome Mr. William Lannigan climbed through a window into a room of a San Fernando boarding house where Mr. William Stack was sleeping. A fight ensued, culminating in the beating of Mr. Stack. When the boarding house cook heard Mr. Stack's cries, he entered the room to find him on the floor, his face covered with blood. The cook asked Mr. Lannigan, who was still in the room, what had happened. Mr. Lannigan said that Mr. Stack had called him a vulgar name and that no one called him such names and he would do it all over again.

Medical assistance and a deputy were called, and Mr. Lannigan was taken to the justice of the peace – which was George. Mr. Lannigan pleaded guilty, George fined him $20 - 2023 equivalent of about $640 - and he was released. Mr. Stack was not in good enough physical condition to appear in court and attest to his side of the story. Later in the day, Mr. Stack died and Mr. Lannigan was arrested and taken to the county jail.

A reporter visited the jailed man and said of Mr. Lannigan, "He possesses a very disagreeable countenance, his eyes denoting much wickedness."

The newspapers were abuzz with details of the case and the subject of the quarrel was attributed to several things; one theory was that it was a disagreement on politics, and another to Mr. Stack being annoyed by the lighting of a candle.

Figure 50: The Los Angeles Evening Express, *November 8, 1888. Courtesy of Newspapers.com.*

Mr. Lannigan was charged with murder and pleaded not guilty. The trial began on January 24, 1889, and George was one of many witnesses called. On February 8, 1889, William Lannigan was found guilty of manslaughter and sentenced to eight years in Folsom Prison.

In 1891, George and Mary sold some of their land to her son George. In 1892, George and Mary sold land they'd purchased in San Fernando, California for $1,250 - the 2023 equivalent of about $42,000, and moved to Bakersfield, Kern County, California.

Finally, the days of land purchases, deals and constant moving were over. Bakersfield, California would be their last home. George was now seventy-four years old.

CHAPTER 11
DEATH OF A PIONEER

George had been in failing health, so he and Mary went to San Luis Obispo, California to take in the warm mineral spring baths there. He ultimately contracted both pneumonia and typhoid fever. Dangerously sick, they went to son Miles' home in Tulare, California in the first days of September 1895. George was reported to be feeling better on September 4, 1895, but the next day, he passed away at Miles' home.

The following article, entitled, "Death of a Pioneer," appeared in the Tulare *Advance-Register* on September 6, 1895:

George M. Holaday, whose sickness has been mentioned in these columns died last night. He was a pioneer who found contentment in advance of civilization. He resided in Iowa at the time when government land was a drug, and once held title to 2400 acres of Hawkeye soil which made him a plutocrat at that time. But he enjoyed trading and moving more than waiting for development and advance of prices, so no fortune was gained from landholdings which have since become valuable. He came to California in the gold stampede of 1850 and spent some months in the placer mines. He then returned to Iowa, to be caught later in the rush to Pike's Peak. After tiring of Colorado mining he drifted from point to point of the wild west, dropping down in Arizona in time to be seated a member of Arizona's first territorial legislature. He removed to southern California, serving as Justice of the Peace for a number of years at Santa Ana. Two years ago he settled on a colony tract near Bakersfield, which place was his home at the time of his death. A month or six weeks ago, not being well, he drove with his wife over to San Luis Obispo to camp and take baths. Here he took cold which resulted in a combination of pneumonia and typhoid fever. They reached Tulare last Sunday night, the old gentleman's desire being to see his son, who resides here. He was given the best of care and medical attention, but the case was believed to be hopeless from the start.

Deceased had a wide acquaintance in California, having spent many years in various counties. He was 77 years old.

In 1890, George received a lengthy biography in *An Illustrated History of Southern California*. There are some errors and many omissions, which will be briefly discussed following the article. I believe George himself was the source of the information. It is printed here without edits, but with added paragraph breaks that were not in the original writing. The reader will be able to recognize the discrepancies and omissions of the following writing as compared to what has been written up to this point.

George M. Holaday, a farmer in Westminster colony, was born October 8, 1818, a son of Samuel and Dollie (Meacham) Holaday: his father a native of Orange County, North Carolina and mother, of Guilford County, same State; they moved to Indiana in 1812. George M., the third in their family of eight children, started out for himself in the world at the age of twenty-one years.

In 1842 he moved to Henry County, Iowa, and from there to Keokuk County, same State, where he remained until 1850. March 12, that year, he left St. Joseph, Missouri, for California, with ox teams, and arrived at Placerville June 12. After a sojourn at the latter place until March, 1851, he went to San Francisco and started thence with a company to the new mines in the north; but about four days after they started their vessel was wrecked and they returned to San Francisco.

Mr. Holaday then went to Sacramento, bought a wagon and a yoke of cattle and went to the Trinity river gold mines; but his success there was not sufficient to justify his remaining, and he returned to Sacramento and hired men to cut and bale wild oats in Napa valley. He had 200 tons cut with an old-fashioned scythe, baled it and shipped it across the Suisan bay and up the river to Sacramento city, where he had a half interest in a feed and sale stable, with James Buckner, on J and Twelfth streets. What hay they could not use they hauled to the mines and sold.

In the fall of 1851 Mr. Holaday located a ranch on the south side of the Sacramento river six miles below Colusa, - a timer section which he supposed to be Government land, - and hired men to cut large quantities of wood, for which he found a ready sale to steamers at $8 per cord. In the fall of 1852 he was notified to leave that place, as it was grant land. There were then about 300 settlers improving it.

One of the owners, Dr. Stoddard, landed at Mr. Holaday's

place from San Francisco to take possession, which was refused by the settlers, over a hundred of whom immediately gathered at that point and elected Mr. Holaday captain. The first thing they determined to do was to get the Doctor out. Mr. Holaday agreed to accomplish the task with a picked lot of men. They marched two and two in a column until they reached the house of John Fitch, where Dr. Stoddard was, about midnight. Holaday placed a guard of four men at each door and window with instructions to allow no one to pass in or out, took four true men, called up Mr. Fitch, who knew his voice and arose and let them in, not knowing his business. The Captain with his men entered the room of Dr. Stoddard, who at first began to show signs of fighting; but as soon as he saw the situation he quietly gave himself up, and Captain Holaday informed him of his mission, assuring him that not even a hair of his head should be touched. They took him and his effects down to the river bank, "the worst-scared man you ever saw;" and he begged to be kept there until morning.

Holaday took a vote from the crowd, which determined that he should be put over the river into Sutter County, - in the midst of a dense thicket inhabited only by wild beasts, even grizzly bears. The vanquished Doctor hailed the steamer next morning and returned to San Francisco, where he reported the matter to the United States Deputy Marshal. A man named Douglass was sent up with injunction papers.

On meeting Captain Holaday they had an argument, wherein all the blame was laid upon Holaday. He reported to the grand jury at San Francisco, who found a bill against Holaday, and Douglass was sent back with four policemen to arrest the indicted man. Holaday was taken to San Francisco, excitement ran high and the newspapers were sensational with the progress of the case. The trial was postponed, matters cooled down, Holaday went to trial, and he and Douglass became good friends by this time, Douglass giving him his own bed in the station house in which to sleep, never offering to imprison him. Holaday's testimony was taken in court, but not that of any other witnesses, and the court fined him to the extent of the law, the result being a loss to him of over $900. In the meantime, while a prisoner, Mr. Holaday sold his ranch, the 400 cords of wood he had on hand, all his stock, and returned to the Atlantic States.

In June 1853, he went back to Iowa and bought 3,000 acres of land in Adair County, Iowa, and followed farming and stock-raising there until 1856; then until 1859 he was at Fort Des Moines, and then until 1860 at Winterset, Madison County, Iowa, when he went to Pike's Peak, on a mining expedition. In 1862 he came on to Salt Lake, remained there two months, and then came to California; stopped eight months in Sacramento, engaged in the hotel business. October 8, 1863, he went to Arizona Territory, ran a whisky mill and boarding house, engaged for three years in the whisky trade at Prescott; in 1867 he went to Sonoma County and kept a bar and hotel there six months; next in 1868 he moved to Orange County, first renting a tract of land; next he took up land in the Los Bolsas tract in 1872, and for nine years followed farming there; and finally he bought a ranch in the tract of the Westminster colony.

Politically he is a Republican. In 1853 he was County Judge of Adair County, Iowa, for two years; at Fort Des Moines he was Justice of the Peace in 1857-58; he was also, while in Arizona, a member of the House of Representatives, aiding in the enactment of Territorial laws; in 1864 he was Speaker of *the House pro tem; and here in Orange County he has been Justice of the Peace several terms, also at San Fernando three years, where he owns valuable property. He is a member of the Holiness Church and an earnest Christian gentleman. He has been a wanderer for many years, but is now settled in a quiet home, where he expects to spend the evening of life, free from the rush and excitement of a public career, etc.*

Mr. Holaday was married in 1868, in San Francisco, to Mrs. Mary E. Finley, a native of Missouri, and a daughter of Erwin Robinson.

A few notable observations regarding this article:

1. There is no mention of his marriage to Lydia, nor of their children. There is also no mention of Elvira, their daughter Arizona, their deaths and their (still living) son George Washington.
2. The entire Trinity River horse theft adventure is left out.
3. The "Squatter Holliday" debacle did not include the "dirty details" about George attacking United States Deputy Marshal Douglass. In fact, it is painted to make George appear to be something of a victim in the affair.
4. The mention of George purchasing 3,000 acres of land in Adair County, Iowa is in question. George did purchase a great deal of land, but 3,000 acres may be an exaggeration.

George was buried in the Tulare Public Cemetery in Tulare, California. I have not found any information regarding his funeral, and no will has been located. His grave marker is simple and spells his middle name as "Mechem," which was also used as an alternative to "Meacham" in years past. I have been told that George's plot was purchased by Mary, and his marker was purchased by second great grandson, Thomas A. Raasch, Jr., decades after George's death. The cemetery recently informed me that they have no record of who purchased the plot or marker, nor when the marker was installed.

Per the cemetery, as of January 2025, the three plots beside George are empty and owned by George and Lydia's great grandson, Leroy C. Holaday, who passed away in 1974. These plots pass to the next of kin, but if no one comes forward, the cemetery will eventually reclaim them. If you are a relative, here is your chance to be buried beside George. ☺

Mary Holaday seems to disappear after George's death, but there is a Mary E. "Halliday" on the 1900 United States Federal Census as an inmate at the Agnews State Hospital for the Insane in Santa Clara, California. Like our Mary, she was born in Tennessee, but it lists her birth year as 1837, rather than 1833. Mary "Halliday" was listed as being the mother of three living children and eight children altogether. How many of Mary Holaday's children were living in 1900 is unknown, but at least two. Our Mary had six biological children and three step children if George W. Holaday is included. Is this our Mary? In the San Francisco earthquake of 1906, the main building of the asylum collapsed, killing 112 people. Sheriff William White, near the asylum at the time, described the scene saying, "Scores of insane persons were running about in the grounds, unwatched and uncared for." Was Mary among them, was she already dead, or was she ever even there at all? Her final resting place, and when she went to it, will likely remain unknown.

George was blessed with 13 children, at least 50 grandchildren, and more than 100 great-grandchildren, yet he knew few of them. His life was a saga of chasing gold and dreams, but it came at a high cost. While pursuing his ambitions, he missed the simple joys of witnessing his children's marriages and the arrival of grandchildren, depriving them, as well as himself, of cherished familial connections. One can't help but wonder if he ever questioned the worth of his endeavors.

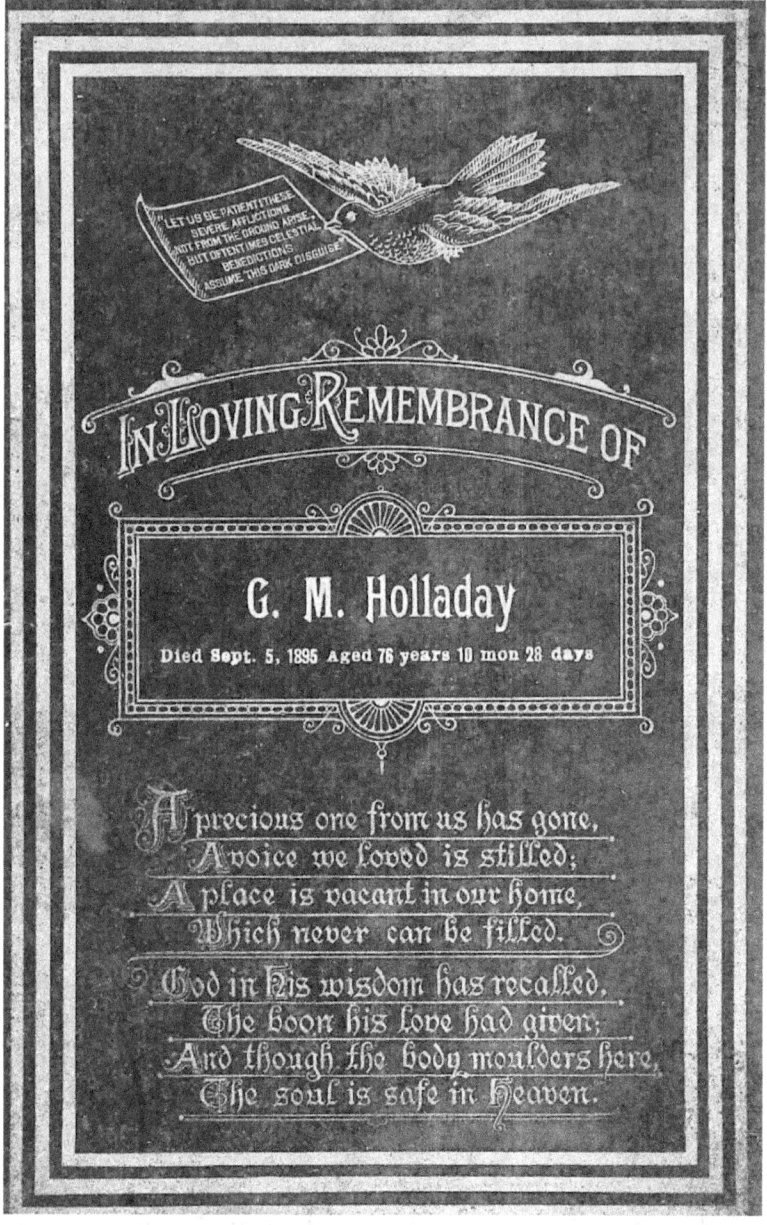

Figure 51: George M. Holaday's funeral cabinet card. Source unknown.

CHAPTER 12
LYDIA HOLLINGSWORTH HOLADAY

Her counsel and example to her children were priceless and they have always reverenced her character and true religious faith. Her long life was unfailingly helpful and unselfish, charitable and steadfast.

In 1860, it was a scandalous matter when a husband abandoned his family, especially after taking a mistress and fathering a child. Such topics would have been spoken of only in hushed whispers. That is likely why tracing it all has been quite a challenge. Lydia, however, handled her hardships with great aplomb and grace. She surely cried her share of tears when she lost her Quaker faith, lost her two young children, lost her husband, and sent her son to war, but she remained steadfast and faithful. She never remarried, nor filed for divorce.

In 1868, Lydia went to live with her son William in Greenfield, Iowa, along with her daughters Pauline and Ellen. After William married, Lydia went to live with her son Samuel and his family in Massena, Iowa. In 1886, she went to Texas to live with her daughter

Ellen. Ellen died in 1891, so Lydia returned to Winterset. She lived with daughter Caroline most of the time from that point forward.

Her children grew up to lead full and industrious lives. The older children had at least known their father for a part of their lives, but the youngest, Henry Delano, never knew his father.

In 1909, Caroline hosted a luncheon at her home. The rule of the invitees was that each were at least fifty years of age, and each had lived in Winterset, Iowa for fifty years or more. It was an occasion to reminisce earlier times and the changes in living since then. The *Winterset Madisonian* said the following about Lydia: "Lydia Holaday, who is nearing the advanced age of ninety years. Her pleasure in listening to and relating some of the incidents of long ago can scarcely be told. It has been her privilege to live and be a part of the early life of this community and time has dealt gently with her. Her memory is still good and she is permitted to enjoy the companionship of old-time friends and to reflect with pleasure on the associations of a half century ago, a privilege accorded to but few." Oh, to be a fly on the wall in that room!

Lydia passed away at Caroline's home in Winterset on July 8, 1911. She had suffered a slight fall two weeks prior, but had been in failing health for some time. The cause of death listed on her death certificate was "senility."

In Lydia's will, filed May 20, 1897, she left a sum of $2,500 to her children and all were named in the will. She did not include any worldly possessions. She indicated that if she were to become "practically helpless, requiring extraordinary care, attention and expense" and that she remain that way for a number of years, that Caroline should have and retain the full amount of $2,500. She made no special requests in her will, other than having a "suitable monument" erected at the place of her burial.

Lydia's estate was insolvent upon her death.

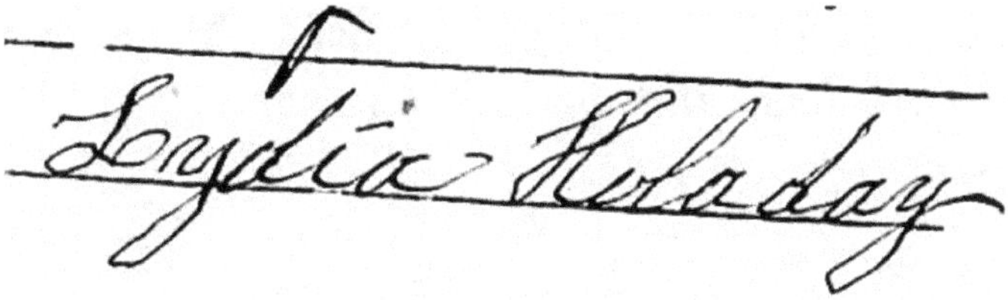

Figure 52: Lydia's signature

Lydia outlived all of her siblings, with the exception of Ruth Jane (Hollingsworth) Witcher, the youngest sibling. Her obituary, printed in the *Winterset Reporter* on July 20, 1911, exactly as originally printed:

Mrs. Lydia Hollingsworth Holaday, one of the oldest residents of Madison County, died last Saturday evening at 8:30 o'clock, at the residence of her daughter, Mrs. Caroline Murray, on west Green street. For a year Mrs. Holaday had been in failing health from the infirmities of age, though no specific disease had attacked her splendid constitution. For over two weeks she had been suffering from the results of a slight fall, and from the intense heat, so that the end occurred more suddenly than expected.

The funeral services were held Monday morning at 10:00 o'clock from Mrs. Murray's residence. They were conducted by the Reverend J.H. Stewart, of the First Baptist church. Though she had outlived nearly all her close acquaintances, the affection in which she was held was shown by the numerous gifts of flowers which lightened the gloom of the occasion.

The pastor paid a fine tribute of appreciation to the memory of one so well fitted from her life to serve as a model of Christian faith. Misses Edith Hyder and Jean Cash and Dr.

Charles Leech and Glenn Tate sang "Abide With Me" and "The Home of the Soul." The interment ceremony at the cemetery was very brief.

The majority of Mrs. Holaday's relatives live too far away to arrive in time for the service. Those who were present were: Mrs. Royal Brown, of Greenfield, Mrs. Caroline Murray, of Winterset, daughters; William Holaday, of Greenfield, Henry Holaday, of Massena, and Milton Holaday, of Council Bluffs, sons: Mrs. Elizabeth Murray Newman, of Winterset, Mrs. James Taylor, of Des Moines, granddaughters: Mrs. Rebecca Hollingsworth Delong, niece: and Mrs. Raymond Waldron, of Winterset, grandniece.

Lydia Hollingsworth Holaday was born in Union County, Indiana, November 28, 1819, so she was close to 92 years of age at the time of her demise. Her ancestors were a Quaker family, prominent in the history of Pennsylvania, Indiana, Illinois and Iowa as pioneers and nation builders. Born in the Friends' faith, she was the greater part of her life unable to attend a church of her belief, yet she lived always according to its truest creedal spirit, being a deep and untiring reader of the Bible, and a searcher for its hidden and inspired meanings.

Her early life was spent near Kokomo, Indiana, and at Danville, Illinois, where her father was a land-owner, and a progressive citizen, honored and beloved by his fellows. They early joined the westward march of the "path-finders," coming to Iowa in 1841. One brother, Dr. Wm. Hollingsworth, settled at Washington, Iowa; another Hon. Jeremiah Hollingsworth, located at Richland, was a member of the Iowa Constitutional Assembly, and a framer and signer of the state constitution of this state. Mrs. Holaday was one of a family of twelve children, only one of whom, Mrs. Ruth Wicher, has survived her.

At the age of 19, Mrs. Holaday was married to George Holaday, afterward a resident of Winterset, owner of the St. Nicholas hotel and judge of Adair County. The young people cleared a farm in Keokuk County, living near Richland for several years. In 1854 they moved to Adair County and in 1859 to Winterset. Here Mrs. Holaday spent most of her long life, after the death of Senator B.F. Murray living constantly with her daughter, Mrs. Caroline Murray.

Of the eleven children born to Mrs. Holaday two died in infancy: her oldest son, Samuel, died six years ago at Massena, Iowa: one daughter, Ellen, died twenty years ago in Denison, Texas: her second son, Miles, lives at Tulare, California. Milton, at Council Bluffs: William, at Greenfield: Henry, near Massena, Iowa: her daughters, Mrs. Emily Brown, at Greenfield: Mrs. Pauline Dabney, at Oakland, California: and Mrs. Caroline Murray, Winterset.

Her counsel and example to her children were priceless and they have always reverenced her character and true religious faith. Her long life was unfailingly helpful and unselfish, charitable and steadfast.

Lydia is buried in the Winterset City Cemetery in Winterset, Iowa. Her headstone is a modest gray marble inscribed simply:

Lydia Holaday
Nov. 23, 1819
July 8, 1911

Lydias parents

EZEKIEL HOLLINGSWORTH (of Joseph, of George, of Abraham, of Thomas, of Valentine Sr.) born: 1781, SC; died: about 1843, Richland, IA; mar 1: JANE HOLLINGSWORTH, daughter of George Hollingsworth and Jane Henry, 1802, SC; born: 1783, Saluda, SC; died: between 1825-1836, IN; mar 2: DOLLY MEACHAM, 10 May 1837, born: 24 Oct 1793, Chatham, NC; died: after 1845.

Lydia's siblings

ZEBULON HOLLINGSWORTH, born: 1805, SC; died: 21 Jan 1878, Madison County, IA; mar: ELIZA KARR, 15 Apr 1834, Vermilion, IL; born: 02 Jun 1816, OH; died: 11 May 1893, Winterset, IA. Children: Elbert White, Rebecca Jane, Katherine, Amanda E., Mahundry.

MARY HOLLINGSWORTH, born: 1808; died: 24 Mar 1867, Richland, IA

JEREMIAH HOLLINGSWORTH, born: 25 Feb 1809, Union Co., IN; died: 25 May 1887, Richland, IA; mar: CATHERINE AMOS, daughter of William Amos and Margret Barnett, 05 Apr 1831, Vermilion, IL; born: 18 Feb 1806, Bourbon County, KY; died: 09 Oct 1889, Richland, IA. Children: Margaret, Jane, Miles, Amos, Asberry, Albert E., Eliza, Emily, America, Amanda, John Wesley, Julia. Eliza and Emily were twins, as were American and Amanda.

MAHUNDRY HOLLINGSWORTH, born: 1810, Union Co, IN. died: before 1880; mar: NANCY ALICE WOLF, born: about 1828, OH. Children: Ida Belle, Miles William, Charles, Edwin.

MILES HOLLINGSWORTH, born: 1811, Dearborn County, IN; died: 1878, Grass Valley, CA; mar: SARAH DUNN, 01 Aug 1866, Virginia City, NV

CYNTHIA ANN HOLLINGSWORTH, born: 12 Jan 1814, possibly - Cynthiana, IN; died: 24 Jan 1873, Clayton, IA; mar: HORACE NEWTON BAGLEY SR., son of John E. Bagley and Jerusha Burroughs, 29 Jul 1846, Keokuk County, IA; born: 22 Sep 1811, Brookfield, VT; died: 23 Jul 1914, Lincoln, NE. Children: John Ezekiel, Jerusha Jane, Mary Amelia, Tryphena Ann, Horace Newton.

JOHN HOLLINGSWORTH, born: 1816, IN; died: 18 Aug 1854, Keokuk County, IA; mar: JANE HOLADAY, daughter of Samuel Holaday and Dolly Meacham, 16 Nov 1837, Vermillion, IN; born: 20 Jan 1821, Orange County, IN; died: 1880, Manning, IA. Children: Elias, Frances Jane, George Edwin

WILLIAM HOLLINGSWORTH DR., born: 14 Nov 1817, Union Co, IN; died: 10 Apr 1908, Dutch Creek, Washington, IA; mar: MARY ANN SINGMASTER, 30 Mar 1856, Washington, IA; born: 06 Jan 1834, Millerstown, PA; died: 02 May 1922, Washington, IA. Children: Ada, Duane, Berthine, Henry, Voline, Della Pauline, Livingston, Clarence.

ELIAS HOLLINGSWORTH, born: 24 Aug 1823, IN; died: 04 Feb 1901, SD; mar: HESTER ANN PALMER, born: 23 Jan 1826, IL; died: 28 Apr 1895, SD. Children: Frances Ellen, Caroline Augusta, Landon Miles, Dorman M., David Palmer, Cynthia Marcella, Lydia Letitia.

ELIZA HOLLINGSWORTH, born: 24 Aug 1823, IN; died: 30 Nov 1855, Portland, OR; mar: LOUIS LIESER, 03 Nov 1842, Henry Co., IA; born: about 1818, Germany; died: 05 Jun 1907, Clark, WA. Child: Henry Clay.

RUTH JANE HOLLINGSWORTH, born: 25 Aug 1825, Vermillion County, IN; died: 12 Mar 1915, Sturgis, SD; mar: NATHANIEL LOVELACE WITCHER, 08 Jul 1847, Iowa County, WI Territory; born: 22 May 1821, VA; died: 11 Nov 1895, Sturgis, SD. Children: Ephraim, Elizabeth Ellen, Martha Jane, Kate Alice, John Frank, Nathaniel Edgar, Henry Clay, Winifred.

Figure 53: Four generation photo circa 1897. From left to right, adults: Lydia (Hollingsworth) Holaday, Caroline (Holaday) Murray, Lenore Kate (Murray) Weirick. The child is Lenore's daughter, Maud Helen Weirick. Image courtesy of Jill Foster Livingston, George and Lydia's third great granddaughter.

Figure 54: Maud Helen (Weirick) Foster on her wedding day in Hollywood, California in 1920. Image courtesy of Jill Foster Livingston.

CHAPTER 13
GEORGE & LYDIA'S CHILDREN

SAMUEL MEACHAM HOLADAY

Samuel was born on November 8, 1839 in Vermillion County, Indiana. He married Almyra Root on December 14, 1863 in Lewis Township, Cass County, Iowa and they had ten children together. Their first-born, a daughter named Gertrude, "Gertie," was George and Lydia's first grandchild. A son named George, born in 1869, died at age ten after being accidentally run over by a wagon wheel. Their sixth born child, Roy William, was this author's great grandfather. Their ninth child, Ethel, died as a toddler.

Roy William was a well-known and highly respected man. His daughter Marjorie wrote the following:

He had no enemies and had an 80-car funeral procession, the largest number anyone could recall for that time. He was a staunch Republican who loved to talk politics. He was very much a non-conformist. He was the director of the one-

room rural school called Whitneyville, which sat on an acre of land which laid on one corner of a crossroads down the hill from the farmhouse where the family lived. At one time, he had it painted red, which was not well accepted and the county superintendent of schools requested it be returned to white, which it was.

Roy had great mechanical abilities, craftmanship, an ear for music. He played the Jew's Harp and the harmonica. He was a nice-looking man with brown hair and blue eyes. He liked beer, but never at the family home. He was an even tempered and kindly man.

In June 1867, Samuel and Almyra moved from Madison to Cass County, Iowa and bought the town plat of Whitneyville. Samuel then bought his farm of 200 acres on section nine and improved the land, making it one of the best farms in the county.

Figure 55: Samuel Meacham Holaday family. From left to right bottom: Myra, Jesse. 2nd row: Gertrude, Almyra, Samuel, Blanche. Standing: Thaddeus, Harry, Roy, Charles

He organized Massena Township, which was constituted on June 11, 1870. Samuel became the justice of the peace and assessor in the fall election of 1870. He was the first secretary of the Massena Township school board.

A snippet of Samuel's diary in *The History of Cass County*:

May 8, 1861, we had a very pleasant day. The wind had layed, and it was not too hot. Our brother campers having several of the female sex along, complained very much about profane language that was used by our company. We camped in a small town called Whitneyville. We met with our friend, Frank Whitney, who invited us to supper, and introduced us to his wife, and treated us to the whisky.

After supper was over, we chatted by the fire and happened to see our cattle starting off down the road toward home. We started after them, and were obliged to follow them about six miles before we could overtake them.

The morning of May 9 brought a pleasant day, and a pleasant night's rest was finished. After breakfast we had the pleasure of seeing two hundred United States troops pass in uniform and marching order. They were from Fort Randall, Dakota Territory. About the middle of the day, we had a rain, which was steady for about four hours, but not very hard. Our things were not very wet. At night we arrived at the Nishnabotna, in Cass County, and camped in the bottom north of town. There were several wagons camped in the bottom. We had considerable fun swimming the cattle across the river to grass, and had some music of violins and songs in the evening after supper. We had boiled one of our pigs, of which I partook of so freely that I was sick for some time afterward.

On the morning of May 10, the roads being soft after the rain, and the weather rather cool, we made a very good day's drive. We took what is called the right hand, or ridge road from Lewis, and left our fellow travelers. In the afternoon, I shot a prairie chicken and had a good old time cooking it, as it was older than Noah himself. In the evening, we camped upon the west fork of the Nishnabotna, a beautiful valley, surrounded on all sides by timber.[12]

From the *History of Cass County*: "He has been an honorable and upright man in the county, and has been honored by the citizens as secretary of the Board of Trustees, a member of the School Board and has been treasurer and assessor of the township. He is one of the prominent men of the township and is highly esteemed by the more substantial class of the county."

Alymra (Root) Holaday was the daughter of Azariah Z. Root, Jr. (Nov. 23, 1790 – Nov. 18 1873) and Mariah "Myra" Skeels (Sep. 24, 1796 – Feb. 12, 1861). Azariah served in the War of 1812. He came to Madison County, Iowa in 1853 and soon after, moved to Adair County, eventually settling in Fontanelle, Iowa. He was the Adair County judge from 1861 to 1864 and the postmaster in Fontanelle in 1862. His only son, Abner, served in the Civil War and was the first sheriff of Adair County, as well as serving as the township assessor and a member of the school board. Azariah, Mariah, and Abner are buried in the Bryant Cemetery in Fontanelle, Iowa.

Her grandfather, Col. Azariah Z. Root Sr., (Dec. 20, 1762 – Dec.

---

[12] The greater prairie chicken, a medium sized bird and native to the Midwest, was once the most abundant game bird across the tallgrass prairies of Iowa. They were sometimes called "boomers," and are similar to a domesticated chicken in shape and size. As more prairie land was converted to row crops, the population began to decline. Overhunting also contributed to their eventual extinction. There are now fewer than one hundred greater prairie chickens in Iowa.

31, 1851) served in the Revolutionary War and was present at the hanging of spy Major John Andre. He was under the command of General George Washington for a short time. In his 1832 pension application, he wrote, "... I next went to West Point and from there to Tappan Bay where I entered my company and regiment and where we were under the command of General Washington, where headquarters were at Orange Tavern." He also served in the war of 1812 and attained the rank of Colonel.

Her great grandfather, Captain Eli Root (Feb. 27, 1731 – Oct. 23, 1804), was a legislator and a Revolutionary War patriot. This author is a member of the Daughters of the American Revolution through this line.

Samuel died on March 29, 1906 and Almyra died on October 31, 1914 in Massena, Cass County, Iowa. They are buried together at the Massena Cemetery.

See descendant information on page 191 .

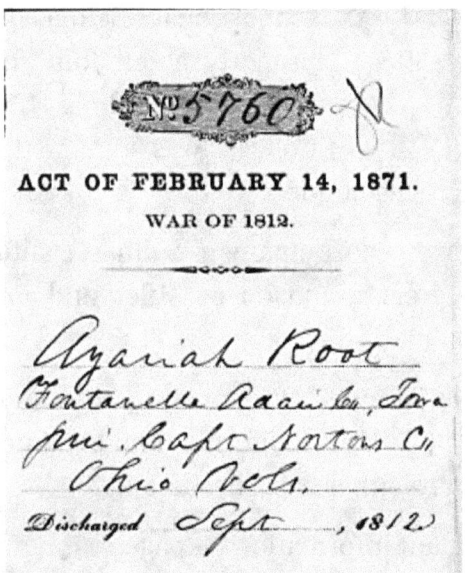

Figure 56: Azariah Root Jr., United States War of 1812 Pension Files, 1812-1815, The National Archives, Catalog ID 564415, record group 15

MILES HOLADAY

Miles was born on March 20, 1841 in Keokuk County, Iowa. Miles and Frances J. "Fannie" Mann were married on January 16, 1868 in Otoe County, Nebraska and had nine children together. Their first three children were born in Nebraska and the rest in California. They eventually settled in Tulare, California, owning and running a dairy and poultry ranch.

Figure 57: Nathan Andrew Holaday

Their son Nathan Andrew moved to Salinas, California in 1896 and was one of the first lettuce growers. He was actively involved in politics and local affairs. Nathan's son Miles Eugene continued the family farming tradition.

Miles Eugene married Marie T. Hartnell, whose grandfather William Edward Hartnell, (1798 – 1854) opened a school near Salinas in 1834 on his property about four miles southeast of present-day Salinas. The Salinas Junior College was renamed Hartnell Junior College in 1948 in his honor.

The Holaday Seed Company in Salinas, California is today run by the second great grandson of Miles and Frances J. (Mann) Holaday.

Miles passed away on December 14, 1916 and Frances died on June 22, 1923 in Tulare, California, and are buried in the Tulare Public Cemetery. Neither has a headstone.

See descendant information on page 195.

JOHN MILTON HOLADAY

John Milton was born in Richland, Keokuk County, Iowa in September 1842. He was blue eyed with sandy colored hair, and went by "Milt." He served in the Civil War, enlisting on January 1, 1862. He was severely wounded in the left leg at The Battle of Pea Ridge, Arkansas on March 7, 1862 and discharged.

He returned to Winterset, Iowa and began a long newspaper and writing career, to become a well-known and respected newspaper man. In the summer of 1863, the *Cass County Gazette* of Lewis, Iowa passed into his hands and he changed its politics to Republican. He also changed the motto to "Westward Ho!" The paper under John Milton's management was said to be "exceedingly spicy" and "too prone to call things by their right names to be popular."

In 1868, he was writing a regular column, in which he referred to himself as "ye Local." He mentioned his mother in his column, saying, "That cheerful and vigorous gal of 49, Lydia Holaday, known extensively as the mother of 'ye Local' and of other less noted chaps, passed westward on Tuesday night's stage, on her way to her Cass County farm. Her habitual smiles in all places and circumstances – her native bent in telling the truth, in opposing horse races and whisky, had much to do in the philosophical and brilliant qualities inherited by ye Local!"

John Milton was seen as a somewhat odd character, with beliefs that raised eyebrows at times, but he was still highly respected. One magazine article he wrote in the *Scientific American* dealt with the "evils" of coffee drinking.

Figure 58: John Milton Holaday's Certificate of Disability for Discharge

John Milton married Mary Kinman about 1871 in either Iowa or Nebraska. Their first child, Will Tipton Holaday, was born on February 11, 1872.

In July 1874, Mary attempted suicide by taking a spoonful of arsenic. After falling unconscious, medical help was called and she was revived. She gave no reason for her attempt.

On October 27, 1876 in Council Bluffs, Iowa, John and Mary's four-year-old son Will Tipton died of "Membranous Croup," more commonly known as Diphtheria, after an illness of just a few days. The vaccine for Diphtheria was many decades away from being developed. The October 28, 1876 obituary in the Council Bluffs *Daily Nonpareil* said, "The little sufferer was conscious to the last, bearing his intense sufferings with a heroism of one of maturer years to the end, when he passed peacefully and without a struggle to the land beyond the gateway of the grave."

The funeral was held at their home, which was customary of the time. He was buried in the Fairview Cemetery in Council Bluffs, Iowa. No headstone has been located.

On April 14, 1877, Mary gave birth to their second child, a daughter named Florence, in Omaha, Nebraska.

John Milton and Mary divorced about 1880. Mary subsequently wed Eugene Street on April 25, 1881. Eugene was the son of Asenath, George M. Holaday's sister, making him John Milton's first cousin. Eugene and Mary also divorced, with the divorce being finalized on June 19, 1888.

Florence married Robert Valentine Weicker on August 7, 1895 in Denver, Colorado. Robert started the Weicker Transfer and Storage Company in Denver with $2.50 and a one-horse wagon, and developed it into a multi-million-dollar company. He died on December 20, 1949, and Florence died on February 29, 1960, both in Denver. They are buried in the Weicker Private Room in a mausoleum at Fairmount Cemetery in Denver. They had two children; Irma and Eunice.

Mary's final marriage was to William R. Stoll in 1917. William died in 1925 and is buried in Ft. Morgan, Colorado. Mary died on February 5, 1928 in Colorado and is buried in the Fairmount Cemetery. She shares a headstone with her sister Jennie.

John Milton finished his life at the Union Printer's Home in Colorado Springs, Colorado. In 1892, the International/National Typographical Union built this facility in Colorado Springs for the care of its ill members. Old typesetters such as John Milton often suffered lung problems as a result of the carbon-based ink used in their profession.

He passed away on January 3, 1926 at age 83 at the Union Printer's Home and is buried in the Union Printers section of its cemetery. His headstone bears "No. 203."

See descendant information on page 197.

CAROLINE HOLADAY

Figure 59: Caroline (Holaday) Murray about 1902. Image courtesy of Jill Foster Livingston, Caroline's second great granddaughter.

Caroline was born on November 27, 1844 in Keokuk County, Iowa. She married Benjamin Franklin "Frank" Murray on November 8, 1864 in Winterset, Iowa after he returned from the Civil War. Caroline and Frank had five children together. Their first-born son, Thaddeus, died in 1869 when he was two years old.

Caroline was a primary school teacher in the Winterset South Ward School, a gifted writer and suffragist. She was the Madison County Recorder for two terms, starting in 1888. In 1897, she was the assistant secretary of the Winterset Equal Suffrage Association.

After her husband's death, she frequently traveled to visit her children who lived in different states. At various times, she also made her home in California. As her mother in Iowa aged, requiring assistance and care, Caroline returned to Winterset, Iowa to be her caregiver.

On Labor Day 1930, when Caroline was eighty-five, she was in a car accident with her granddaughter in Los Angeles, California. Her granddaughter, who had been driving, suffered no injuries. Caroline was injured but was expected to recover. However, she fell into a coma a few days later and passed away on September 11, 1930. Her death certificate lists the cause of death as "exhaustion following severe crushing injury of the chest with multiple fractures of the ribs. Auto accident." She is buried at Forest Lawn Memorial

Park in Glendale, California beside her daughter Elizabeth.

Figure 60: Benjamin Franklin "Frank" Murray

Benjamin, or "Frank" as he was called, was born on August 20, 1838 in Ohio and his family came to Madison County, Iowa about 1854. He studied law from 1857 to 1858 and was admitted to the practice of law in 1859. He volunteered in the Civil War for the Union in the 3rd Regiment, Iowa Infantry, Company G.

He was captured at the Battle of Shiloh, Tennessee on April 6, 1862 and imprisoned, although for some time, he was believed to have been killed. He was taken from one prison to another, as they were driven farther south in retreat. He was initially imprisoned at Corinth, Mississippi, then Tuscaloosa, Alabama and finally, on May 10, 1862, at Montgomery, Alabama. Conditions at Montgomery were deplorable. It was a foul, vermin-abounding cotton depot, 200 feet long and 40 feet wide, without blankets and only hard earth or wood planks as beds. Of the 700 Union soldiers imprisoned there, 198 died from malnutrition and disease.

Frank was traded in a prisoner exchange on May 22, 1862 and sent to the Camp Benton hospital in St. Louis, Missouri. He was diagnosed with a left side hernia and discharged on August 28, 1862. He returned home in exceedingly poor health and severely emaciated. His return was an event in Winterset. His father, Nicholas Murray, laughingly said that the "Rebs" would have "hard work shooting Frank as his legs were so thin a bullet would pass between them."

Frank and Caroline's first child, a daughter they named Lenore, was born in 1865. Another daughter, Maude, would follow in 1868,

Nicholas in 1871, and Elizabeth in 1876.

He was vehemently opposed to Southern sympathizers, i.e., "Copperheads." On August 24, 1865, he and other "Boys in Blue" attended the Soldiers' State Convention at the courthouse, only to find that a majority of the delegates were Copperheads. When it was revealed that although citizens and soldiers were allowed to attend, but only anti-Stone and anti-negro suffrage supporters were entitled to seats, a ruckus ensued.[13] Frank offered a resolution calling for only soldiers to be admitted as members of the convention. He made a short speech, proclaiming that, "So help him God Almighty, he would never sit in council with the rebels and traitors of Iowa," which was met with uproarious applause. When Frank's resolution was deemed out of order, about two thirds of the soldiers from Madison County and other western and central counties withdrew from the convention and relocated to hold their own meeting at Sherman Hall. Only soldiers were allowed to attend the packed facility. They resolved that, "We, the citizen-soldiers of Iowa, never have affiliated, and never will affiliate, with the Copperheads of Iowa, in any political party whatever."

After the war, Frank practiced law. In 1867, he was elected to represent Madison County in the State Legislature. After one term, he was elected state senator.

In June 1876, just before his daughter Elizabeth's birth, Frank

---

[13] William M. Stone, a strong supporter of President Abraham Lincoln, was the sixth governor of Iowa, from 1864 to 1868. He enlisted as a private in the Union Army and was promoted to captain and major of Company B, 3rd Iowa Volunteer Infantry Regiment. He was wounded and taken prisoner. He was promoted to colonel of the Twenty-Second Iowa Volunteer Infantry Regiment and led that unit in the Vicksburg Campaign. He appointed the first female notary public in the United States. He served one term in the Iowa House of Representatives from 1877 to 1878 and was appointed assistant commissioner and commissioner of the United States Land Office. He is buried at Graceland Cemetery in Knoxville, Iowa. Source: Wikipedia

suffered what was likely a stroke. Afterward, his mental health deteriorated to the point that he was institutionalized at the Mount Pleasant, Iowa Insane Asylum, originally known as the Iowa Lunatic Asylum. It was an overcrowded facility that became known to often deliver substandard care.

His diagnosis was "hardening of brain." This condition was usually due to the constriction or blocking of the cerebral arteries. It led to the reduction of the flow of blood to the brain, resulting in damage to neural tissue and loss of mental function(s). Depending on whether or not it was a large blood vessel, a major stroke or cerebral vascular accident could be suffered, leading to not just a confusional state, but to serious and often permanent loss of brain function.

Frank would spend the rest of his life institutionalized. It can't be known how often the family was able to visit him in the asylum, nor how often he was able to make visits home, if at all. It was an approximately 150-mile journey from Winterset to Mt. Pleasant. It would certainly have been a painful, lonely and challenging time for both Frank and Caroline, as well as the children, who now had no father in the home.

In 1890, Frank was transferred to the Clarinda Asylum for the Insane in Clarinda, Page County, Iowa, about ninety miles southwest of Winterset. The Mt. Pleasant facility had become dangerously overcrowded. Clarinda had opened in 1888, the third mental asylum in Iowa at the time. Patients in insane asylums were all too often abused in the name of "treatment" with gruesome procedures, such as lobotomies, electroshock therapy, ice baths and forced drugging. Other issues were improper food and water, starvation, dehydration, abuse, surgeries, and extreme climate.

On May 3, 1890, Caroline had her husband brought home to Winterset, the journey made on a cot. He was very happy to be back home, able to recognize his family and friends, and to converse readily about politics and other news of the day. After several days, however, on May 7, 1890, at the age of fifty-two, he passed away. He was buried in the Winterset City Cemetery.

In his obituary in the *Winterset Madisonian* on May 9, 1890, it was written:

> *But affliction laid its heavy hand upon him. Worse than physical suffering, mental darkness enshadowed him. He became insane, and was sent to an asylum for the insane. There he remained until last week. But his mind became clearer. At last, he seemed quite rational. And last Saturday he was brought home to his family. He was very sick, not able to sit up. His lungs were much affected, and his body, though always of spare build, had become very much emaciated. Mentally, he seemed to have all his old vivacity and cheerfulness. He conversed readily about past and present politics and business, and seemed, as of old, to be thoroughly informed as to the progress of events.*
>
> *He enjoyed himself at home as well as could be expected, much better, he said, than he did at asylum. But his longed-for rest with his family was short. On Wednesday morning early, as the night was breaking into glorious day, his last, lingering hold on life was broken, and he passed from earth.*

Another passage read:

> *Frank, as we all called him, was an unusually promising boy, and early in life became a leader of men. He had hosts of friends who stood by him from first to last. He made an enviable record as a legislator and was prominent and influential. When the dark shadow came upon him, he was more generally known over the state than any citizen of Madison County, and higher political eminence was before*

him but for the calamity that ended all, and but for that there can scarcely be a doubt but that the commonwealth would long ago have called him to its highest political station. His prospects for the future were the brightest. He was a born politician and had the magnetism that enrolled numbers as his followers and friends. He was emphatically an American boy and a self-made man. He had no influential relatives to aid him, and he climbed the ladder by his own merit and exertions.

The article also spoke of Caroline:

Through all these years, all Madison County people know how bravely Mrs. Murray has grappled with misfortune. Left with but little to depend on except her homestead, by teaching school, and taking care of her family when other teachers are usually resting, she has for almost fourteen years kept the old home, and brought up and educated her family till three of her four children have become self-supporting, and able to render her assistance. Two years ago she was elected recorder of Madison County, and is now in the second year of her first term.

Frank's will called for dividing his money between his four children in equal amounts and double to his wife. Each child received $118.90, the equivalent of $3,900 in 2023, and Caroline received $237.81, the equivalent of $7,780.

Daughter Elizabeth would become more like her grandfather George than any other child or grandchild by far, having the same wanderlust that he did. She was a gifted writer, poetess, lecturer, orator and like her mother, a staunch suffragist. She had a very engaging personality. She traveled the world and for a time, achieved worldwide fame. Sadly, she also abandoned her daughter and she also ended up in jail, as her grandfather had. See her Mini

Biography on page 180.

Figure 61: Maude (Murray) Ward

Daughter Maude (Murray) Ward, achieved the impressive feat of being the best paid woman in Los Angeles, California in 1911. She was said to be the only woman at that time making a living by selling lumber in the country.

Maude shared a sad similarity with her grandmother Lydia, however. Maude was also abandoned by her husband just after giving birth. Maude had married Thomas F. Ward, a wealthy lawyer, banker and politician, in 1895.

In April 1901, Mr. Ward embezzled money from the bank where he worked in Le Mars, Iowa and fled to the east coast. He eventually faced an Iowa court, but the punishment was minimal. By then, Maude had moved to California with their newborn son Murray Ward.

Murray became wealthy and influential in Southern California as a high-ranking executive at E.F. Hutton. He married socialite Virginia (Peggy) Leonide Ducommun in 1942. Murray raised Virginia's son, Anthony Converse Taylor, as his own. Murray Ward passed away on January 17, 1985 in Beverly Hills, California.

Maude married again on February 10, 1916, to Daniel Moore Locey in Phoenix, Arizona. He was a millionaire mining magnate with large mining interests in and around Prescott, Arizona. On February 16, 1916, the *Weekly Journal-Miner* said of Maude, "Mrs. Ward is considered one of the most beautiful women in Southern California, where lovely women abound. She has taken a prominent part in the social, club and political life of Los Angeles and vicinity, and is a former president of the Women's Republican League of Los

Angeles County."

By June 1918, the marriage had fallen apart and Maude returned to Los Angeles. She never married again and raised her son as a single mother. She died on August 5, 1952, at age eighty-four, in Los Angeles, California. She was cremated and buried at Forest Lawn Memorial Park in Glendale, California. She shares a marker with her sister Lenore.

Figure 62: Lenore Kate (Murray) Weirick

Daughter Lenore married Emerson Bond Weirick on November 17, 1892 in Winterset. They moved to Montana and had three children. Mr. Weirick was a Montana native who would become a wealthy banker and businessman.

In 1917, Lenore, Emerson and two daughters moved to Hollywood, California, while their son Arthur remained in Montana. They made their home at 6831 Odin Street in Hollywood. Her home, according to a news article, was "among the most beautiful in the Hollywood hillsides, commanding a wonderful view of all the surrounding hills and mountains, covered with stately trees and shrubs. The house is of Spanish architecture, with a patio in the center, with a rose garden, fountain, bamboo trees, Palins and tropical trees, filling the marvelous lawn." The entire neighborhood is gone now and where the home once sat is a parking lot.

Lenore was a well-known club and society woman in Montana, and would continue to be so in California. She and her sister Maude, (not to be confused with Lenore's daughter Maud), would spend a great deal of time together, serving on committees, attending society functions, etc. They would be very close for the rest of their lives.

Lenore passed away on December 22, 1951 in Los Angeles, California at age eighty-five.

Son Nicholas moved to the South, living in several southern cities over the years: Birmingham, Alabama; New Orleans, Louisiana and Macon, Georgia. In 1906, he married Josephine Claudine Dupin, whose parents were born in France. They had one son named Franklin Blair Murray. In about 1927, Nicholas went to live in Los Angeles with his mother and died there on February 17, 1929. He is buried at the Angelus Rosedale Cemetery in Los Angeles. Josephine died on June 27, 1944 in Birmingham, Alabama and is buried in the Oak Hill Cemetery in Birmingham.

See descendant information on page 198.

EMMA CAROLINE HOLADAY

Emma was born on August 16, 1846 in Sigourney, Keokuk County, Iowa. Emma married Royal Oran Brown, of Ohio, on February 6, 1868 in Adair County, Iowa and they had nine children together. She and husband Royal settled in Union Township near Greenfield, Iowa. He was an accountant and land agent and she was a housewife.

In 1863, Royal attended the Western Reserve Eclectic Institute in Ohio when President James A. Garfield was its principal. Garfield would become the twentieth United States President in 1880, but his presidency ended abruptly when he was assassinated in 1881.

Royal's father, Oran E. Brown, was appointed United States Postmaster in Fontanelle, Iowa on January 15, 1866.

Royal was elected Adair County recorder in 1872 and re-elected twice. He was appointed deputy treasurer in 1864.

Emma passed away at age seventy-one on March 26, 1918 and Royal died at age seventy-two on June 4, 1919 – both in Greenfield, Iowa. They are buried together in the Greenfield Cemetery. Emma's twin sister was Ellen Holaday.

See descendant information on page 199.

ELLEN HOLADAY

Ellen was born on August 16, 1846 in Sigourney, Keokuk County, Iowa – the twin of Emma. She remains the most elusive of the Holaday children, as so little is known of her.

She married John Gallagher on February 10, 1882 in Sherman, Texas. It is not known whether they divorced or John passed away, but Ellen married again, to P. Bradley, on November 25, 1889, in Sherman, Texas.

Ellen passed away in Denison, Texas in 1891. It is unknown where she was buried. It is also unknown when either of her husbands died, nor where they were buried. No records have been found to indicate whether or not she had any children.

WILLIAM HOLADAY

William was born on March 25, 1848 in Keokuk County, Iowa. On July 16, 1873, William married Jennett Anna Gaylord in Montgomery County, Iowa and they had four children. William was an auctioneer and stock dealer. They moved to Greenfield, Iowa in about 1880 and remained there for the rest of their lives.

Jennett passed away on March 9, 1926 at age seventy-seven. William passed away at age eighty-three on November 26, 1931. They are buried together at the Greenfield, Iowa cemetery.

Figure 63: William and wife Jennett in front of their home in Greenfield, Iowa. Image courtesy of Sam Holiday, George and Lydia's 2nd great grandson.

See descendant information on page 201.

THOMAS JEFFERSON HOLADAY

Thomas Jefferson was born in Jefferson Township, Adair County, Iowa in the fall of 1854. The township is said to have been named after him. He died in the fall of 1855 in the same place. He was buried along with another child, William Alcorn, in a pasture field on section twenty-six. William died of a rattlesnake bite. The field was plowed over many years ago and there is no marker to indicate where their burials are.

ORPHA HOLADAY

Orpha was born in spring 1856 in Adair County, Iowa and likely died there as well. It is not known where she was buried. The only record she appears on is the Iowa State Census in 1856. She does not appear on the next census in 1860, so she has died by then.

PAULINE HOLADAY

Figure 64: Pauline (Holaday) Dabney. Image courtesy of Drew Dabney.

Pauline was born on June 19, 1857 in Des Moines, Polk County, Iowa. She moved to Winterset, Iowa with her family as a toddler and grew up there.

She was a school teacher in a private home in Madison County prior to the erection of the first school building in 1875. Pauline married Albert Rush Dabney on June 19, 1877 in Winterset, Iowa. They had four children – all daughters.

The Dabney home, built in 1860, is still standing on West Jefferson Street in Winterset. It is a beautifully preserved, nearly 3,000 square foot, two-story brick home.

In 1891, Pauline was elected to serve on an advisory board for Madison County for the American Educational Association. This society placed homeless children in good Christian homes. Those on the advisory boards were to have oversight of any children placed within the county and inform the association in regard to each case.

Albert, Pauline and family moved from Winterset to Oakland, California in 1900. Pauline was very close to her sister Caroline and was with her when Caroline passed away. Caroline's daughter Elizabeth was married at Pauline's home in Oakland.

Pauline passed away on April 9, 1936, at age seventy-nine, in Oakland.

Albert's family had come to Madison County, Iowa from Illinois about 1856, when he was 13 years old. He enlisted in the

13th Iowa Infantry during the Civil War, and served until the regiment was mustered out.

Figure 65: Albert Rush and Pauline (Holaday) Dabney. Image courtesy of Drew Dabney.

He was a lawyer in Iowa and prominent in politics, having been admitted to the bar in 1872. He represented Madison County in the Twentieth and Twenty-first Iowa General Assemblies, 1884 and 1886. In Illinois he served as a state senator from 1884 to 1888. He bought a great deal of real estate in and around Oakland, California, becoming a promoter and investor.

He died on June 12, 1913 at age sixty-eight at his home in Oakland. He left Pauline and daughters sizable holdings. They are both buried at Mountain View Cemetery in Oakland, California, although Pauline is buried in a mausoleum.

Figure 66: Dinner at the Dabney home in California circa 1904. Image courtesy of Drew Dabney.

At head of table: Pauline (Holaday) Dabney, left, and husband Albert Rush Dabney, right. On right, girl sitting: Helen Jane Dabney. To right of girl sitting: Elizabeth Murray. On left, boy sitting: Albert Dabney Schwaner. Next to him on left: Lenore (Dabney) Schwaner.

The following is a likely identification of others in the photo, but is not certain:

To right of Elizabeth Murray: Lenore (Murray) Weirick, Maude (Murray) Ward, Caroline (Holaday) Murray

See descendant information on page 202.

HENRY DELANO HOLADAY

Figure 67: Henry Delano Holaday

Henry was born on April 10, 1860 in Winterset, Madison County, Iowa. Henry married Mary M. Spies on May 10, 1885 in Franklin Township, Cass County, Iowa and they had four children together. He was a farmer and she a housewife. They lived their entire married lives together in Cass County.

He passed away on November 28, 1924 at age sixty-four. The orders of the Masonic and Eastern Star attended.

Mary lived a very long life, passing away at age ninety-nine on June 5, 1963 in Atlantic, Iowa. She was a fifty-year member of the Order of the Eastern Star and held a lifetime membership in the organization.

They are buried together at the Massena Cemetery in Massena, Cass County, Iowa.

See descendant information on page 204.

Figure 68: Mary (Spies) Holaday. Image courtesy of Wayne Barkhousen, George and Lydia's second great grandson.

CHAPTER 14
MINI BIOGRAPHIES OF NOTE

GEORGE WASHINGTON HOLADAY

George's son with Elvira, George Washington Holaday, bore similar physical characteristics as his father: 5'8, light complexion, blue eyes and light hair. He was born on March 2, 1859 in Iowa – most likely in Des Moines. He married Sarah Isabel Atwood on April 27, 1884 in San Bernardino, California and they had four children together. He was a Teamster. They moved to San Diego, California about 1915.

Sarah's parents left Council Bluffs, Iowa in a wagon train on May 29, 1860 to emigrate to California. This was almost exactly the time that George, Elvira and George W. also left Iowa, headed west.

In an article entitled "Covered Wagon Families: Danford Atwood Brought Family From Iowa in 1860," in the *San Bernardino County Sun* on December 7, 1938, we get some interesting insight into Sarah's parents' trip from Iowa westward.

Danford and Jane, with their children, left Council Bluffs on May 29, 1860. Capt. William Guard was the leader. It was his seventh trip across the plains. About 100 wagons left Council

Bluffs in the trip. Each family had two wagons.

...The pioneers crossed the great plains and traveled for days up and down the Platte River to find a place to cross. John Wheeler drove the domestic stock. They crossed and recrossed the Platte River many times. Ten miles a day was considered good. Every night when they would make camp the Indians would gather around for food. During the day they were not seen. Captain Guard could talk a little with the Indians. The Indians would ask if they were Mormons, and the pioneers were told to say that they were 'good Mormons.' The herds of buffalo were as much to be feared as the Indians.

Between the Platte River and Salt Lake, Lucy E. Janney narrowly escaped being carried off by the Indians. One morning just after leaving camp, she and another little girl were trailing the last wagon, walking along barefooted, burying sticks and stones, which they intended to pick up when they came back. Two Indians emerged from the bushes and began chasing them. One of the Indians grabbed Lucy by the feet just as she was jumping into the wagon. Captain Guard saw the Indian and rushed to the scene, where he convinced the Indian that he did not want the little blonde child.

George W. Holaday passed away on January 19, 1926 in San Diego. Sarah died on August 26, 1954 in Los Angeles. He is buried in the Mt. Hope Cemetery in San Diego and Sarah is buried in the mausoleum at Cypress View in San Diego.

It is not known if George M. and his son George W. had a relationship after George W. became an adult.

See descendant information on page 206.

CYNTHIA ANN HOLLINGSWORTH BAGLEY

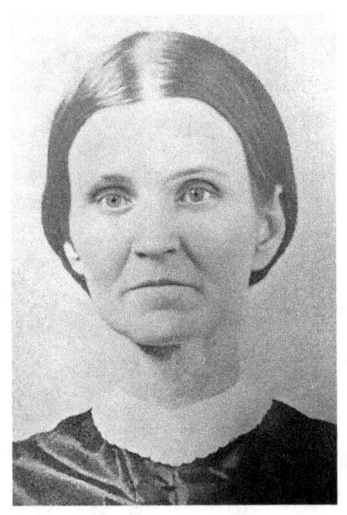

Figure 69: Cynthia (Hollingsworth) Bagley

Cynthia was the second born daughter of Ezekiel and Jane Hollingsworth, born five years before Lydia, on January 12, 1814. The place of Cynthia's birth has been documented as Cynthiana, Posey County, Indiana, but it is a rather curious location. If this is indeed the birth location, the family did not spend much time there and she would have been the only child born there.

Cynthia came to Iowa with the rest of her family in 1840 and settled in Richland, Iowa becoming a school teacher. Her legal name was "Cynthia," but she often went by "Cyntha." The name on her headstone is the latter.

Cynthia loved to write poetry. In 1842, soon after coming to Iowa, she wrote a poem entitled, "On the Beauties of Iowa:"

> *Oh! how beautiful is this place,*
> *How pure and clear the air,*
> *It now appears in a gentle grace*
> *Oh how divinely fair.*
>
> *It calls my attention from my book,*
> *To view its beauties now;*
> *When I upon its beauties look,*
> *My soul and spirits bow.*
>
> *Where I view the waving wood,*
> *I think of power divine,*

I think of an Almighty God,
Which forever shall be mine.

Where I view the landscape wide,
Portrayed in colors fair
And the gentle flowing tide,
I see He is everywhere.

When I hear the sweet birds sing,
I think of worlds on high.
I think of that Eternal spring,
When our souls to God shall fly.

The lofty peak, the spreading vale,
His wonderous power display,
All animate nature tells the tale;
In animate portray.

We can trace Omnipotence,
In all created things;
The shining stars and bright expanse,
A heavenly anthem sings.

All honor to our Father due,
All honor to our God,
He spoke the word, the mountain grew,
And oceans flowed aboard.

All honor is due to our God,
All honor is due the Son;
For He created with His word
And redeemed us with his blood.

On Mount Zion's cross he hung,
On Calvary he died,
Our salvation He has won,
For God is pacified.

Cynthia married Horace Newton Bagley, Sr. on July 29, 1846 in Keokuk County, Iowa. They had five children: John Ezekiel, Jerusha Jane, Mary Amelia, Tryphena Ann and Horace Newton Jr. In the early 1850s they moved to Clayton County, Iowa – about 150 miles north of Richland, Iowa. Horace lived to be 102 years old. Their son John Ezekiel became a prominent and well-respected attorney and judge in Ogden, Utah, and in 1917, was appointed United States Commissioner for the district of Ogden.

Cynthia passed away on January 24, 1873 and is buried in the Giard Cemetery in Farmersburg, Clayton County, Iowa. Horace died on July 23, 1914 and is buried in the Walnut Grove Cemetery in Brownville, Nebraska.

HERBERT JOHNSON

Horace and Cynthia's daughter Mary Amelia married Joseph W. Johnson and they had five sons, the second born being Herbert Hollingsworth Johnson, born in 1878. Herbert attended the University of Nebraska at Lincoln in 1900, where his second cousin, Elizabeth Murray, (Caroline's daughter), was also attending.

Herbert, like his grandmother, was a Quaker and became one of the best-known cartoonists in the country. He was a cartoonist for the *Denver Republican* in 1896, when he was just seventeen. He worked as a freelancer for many years as a cartoonist for the *Saturday Evening Post, Country Gentleman, Life, Colliers* and *LaFollette's*, among others. He never took a single art class. He illustrated over 1,300 cartoons for the *Saturday Evening Post* alone.

He was staunchly opposed to Franklin Roosevelt and the New Deal policies. This led to a new style of cartoons for him, with a new political edginess. He had a sense of humor, however, and was quite witty. One of his quotes:

I have always been temperamentally opposed to the tyranny of vested interests, and at the ripe age of nine, feeling that my personal liberties were being unduly curtailed by the stand-pat policies of the family government adhered to by my parents, I insurged, and ran away from home, hitting the trail for the Black Hills. I returned after a few days to submit to the domestic steam roller.

Herbert married Helen Leticia Turner on January 8, 1908 in Pennsylvania. They had two children: Herberta Hollingsworth and Katherine Turner Johnson. He died on December 4, 1946 in Montgomery County, Pennsylvania. He is buried at the West Laurel Hill Cemetery with his wife, who died on March 23, 1959.

Figure 70: Critical Moments, *a cartoon by Herbert Johnson. The word by the man on the tree is "Taxpayers." The words by the bears are "Old Taxes" and "New Taxes." Library of Congress. Image in the public domain.*

Figure 71: A cartoon by Herbert Johnson. In the circle to the top left, the sign says, "To the poor house." The sign on the pole says, "Taxpayer." In the main body, the text says, "The Congressman who is for economy always and hates to spend the taxpayers' money, but for some reason, always finds it is duty to vote for every grab, junkey, pork barrel and extravagance." Library of Congress. Image in the public domain.

ELIZABETH "BESSIE" MURRAY SHEPHERD

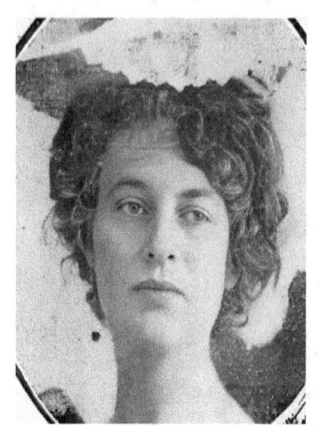

Figure 72: Elizabeth "Bessie" (Murray) Shepherd

George and Lydia's granddaughter Elizabeth Murray, daughter of Benjamin F. and Caroline (Holaday) Murray, was born in Winterset, Iowa on July 30, 1876. She went by "Bessie" until she reached adulthood. Her father never lived in the home with her, as he had taken ill the same month of her birth.

Elizabeth graduated from Winterset High School in 1894, ranking academically at the top of her class. She attended Stanford University in California from 1894 to 1896, so she would have been in the state of California when her grandfather George died, but no doubt was completely unaware of it. At Stanford, she was a substitute on the women's basketball team and she and her winning team appeared in the May 30, 1896 *Harper's Bazaar*. After Stanford, she also attended the University of Nebraska and Northwestern University. She was the first female to place and win a prize in an oratorical contest at the latter.

From an early age, she was passionate about women's suffrage. She was elected president of the Madison County Suffrage Association at just age twenty-one – the youngest county president in the National American Woman Suffrage Association.

She married Charles J. Newman in California, but their marriage ended in divorce after an embarrassing situation in which they defrauded individuals with bogus checks and unpaid debts.

She loved to write and worked as an editor and assistant editor for many magazines. She wrote poetry, short stories and articles. She was boisterous, couldn't sit still and had the same wanderlust as her grandfather, although she never knew him. Her career took off and she became known worldwide.

She was adopted by Lorenzo S. Coffin, an eighty-nine-year-old, wealthy, and well-known philanthropist, when she was thirty-six. It caused a major stir and made nationwide headlines.

Her next and last marriage was to Frank W. Shepherd, a respected politician from Illinois. They had one child together, but Elizabeth soon discovered that motherhood and the life of a wife wasn't for her.

Elizabeth's lavish lifestyle far outstripped her financial means. Though she received support from her mother and sister, it fell short of sustaining her in the way she wanted to live. Her solution was to write bad checks to cover her debts, which only worsened her predicament. In spite of multiple arrests, she persisted, devising an even more elaborate scheme - selling memberships to a fictitious organization. After trying to peddle such a membership to the father of former United States President Harding and actually succeeding in selling one to the Oil Queen of Texas, Elizabeth's duplicity finally caught up to her. Even assuming a new identity of "Elizabeth Tarkington" didn't let her evade the long arm of the law.

She was indicted for "using the mails to defraud" and pleaded guilty. She was sent to Alderson Women's Prison in Alderson, West Virginia, where she served fifteen months. The newspapers exploded with headlines such as, "Her Fame World-Wide, She Now Faces Prison Term," and "Woman Whose Fame Was World-Wide Now Faces Term in Prison for Fraud."

She gave one final interview where she made the last quote that would ever be attributed to her. She said, "I guess I'm through forever. I don't think I'll ever write again. Something inside me has died. If I ever do write it will be under a new name. Elizabeth Murray's career is dead."

After she served her term, she returned to California, where shortly thereafter, her mother died as a result of injuries of a car crash. Elizabeth never wrote again, or at least not under her real name.

She led the rest of her life in obscurity, dying on her birthday, July 30, in 1956 in Los Angeles, California. She is buried in an unmarked grave beside her mother.

Her biography, "Echoes of Ambition," the second book in "The Holadays" series, will be released in 2025. Please see http://www.tallgrassprairiebooks.com for more information.

Figure 73: The San Francisco Examiner, *December 29, 1909, front page. Courtesy of Newspapers.com.*

ARTHUR MURRAY WEIRICK

Figure 74: Arthur Murray Weirick about 1917.

George and Lydia's great grandson Arthur Murray Weirick was born on October 16, 1893 in Helena, Montana. He was the son of Lenore, daughter of Caroline. He applied for the Army Aviation Corps after the outbreak of World War I. He took and passed the examination for the corps and trained in Champaign, Illinois and Mineola, New York, becoming a lieutenant. He was ordered to Europe in September 1917 to complete his final training before entering active service at the front.

When the time came for him to leave for Europe, his father, Emerson B. Weirick, accompanied him to the East Coast to see him off, but his mother Lenore could not bear the deeply emotional send-off. She was terrified that her son was going off to war, never to return.

Arthur was a first lieutenant with the 213th Aero Squadron in France. In March 1918, he wrote a letter home that was published in the Montana *Anaconda Standard*. He said, "As yet I haven't been near the front – don't know what it looks like, but within two or three months from now, after I've learned some of the fine points of fighting at 20,000 feet, I hope to be able to do my bit in making Germany realize that red blood is more powerful than efficiency." He would indeed do "his bit."

In a letter home to his mother in September 1918, he told her, "You can't lose if you play the game right, and by that I mean being true to one's self. Right now I could very likely pick up a good bombproof job rather than go on flying, but throughout life I'd be ashamed of myself, and the more I see of it all over here the plainer is the fact that as a man thinks to himself so is his character, and so will he live. If I took a safe office position over here, I'd be able to go back home and people would say, 'He did his duty,' but throughout my life I'd know deep in my heart that I wasn't a real man because I'd been tried and found wanting. And that, sweet mother, is the way in which I look at things – the way which I want you to feel about me – if I fall here, I fall game, and if I return, I return as deep in your heart you would have your son return."

On October 31, 1918, Arthur and a fellow aviator were reported as missing after being shot down while acting as guard for American bombing planes behind enemy lines in Germany in the Meuse-Argonne campaign in the battle of the Argonne Forest. This campaign was the largest offensive in United States military history, involving 1.2 million American soldiers. It was also the deadliest in the history of the United States Army. The Spanish Flu also played a part in the casualty numbers.

Figure 75: *Weirick Dead in German Hospital.* The Anaconda Standard, *December 12, 1918. Courtesy of Newspapers.com.*

From their home in Hollywood, California, his parents anxiously awaited news that he had been found. Instead, on December 11, 1918, they received the news they most dreaded: Arthur had been killed and had died in a German hospital. Newspapers reported his death widely with headlines such as, "Meets Fate in Aviation Service," and "Butte Boy Is War's Victim."

After grieving for two days, his parents were granted the greatest reprieve they could have ever hoped for. The accounts of his death were in error. He had been shot through the left shoulder, his plane was shot down and crashed, he was taken as a prisoner and sent to a German hospital, but he was alive. The conclusion of the campaign culminated in the armistice of November 11, 1918 that ended World War I, when he was then sent to an American hospital. He lost most of the use of his left arm as the result of his injury.

One can only imagine the overwhelming surge of emotions his parents experienced during the ordeal. His mother Lenore said, "I want every mother who has lost a boy to know that in all my present joy, I feel a tenderness, a sympathy, a depth of understanding for her in the loss she has sustained. That is all that keeps me from being supremely happy these days since that wonderful cable came over the seas, but that knowing and realizing how many mothers suffered as I did for a week and then no cable came – oh, how my heart aches for the broken homes."

Arthur returned home in February 1919. He married his sweetheart Margaret "Jimmy" Mae Lowry on November 17, 1919 in Butte, Montana. She said she had never given up hope on him being alive. After their wedding, headlines ran nationwide, such as, "Montana Beauty Is Bride of Long-Mourned Aviator." A photo of her accompanied one article with the caption, "The most beautiful girl in Montana."

Circa 1950, they moved to Corona, California and lived atop a hill over their orange grove. The couple had two children together: Thomas Lowry (1920 – 1973) and Jane Lowry (1927 – 2018) Weirick.

Arthur died on May 18, 1972 and Margaret died on July 29, 1982 – both in Corona, California. Their ashes were scattered.

EPHRAIM WITCHER

Figure 76: Ruth Jane (Hollingsworth) Witcher.

Ephraim, born in Wisconsin Territory in 1848, was Lydia's nephew; the son of her sister Ruth Jane Hollingsworth. Ruth married Nathaniel Lovelace Witcher on July 8, 1847 in Beetown, Wisconsin Territory. They moved to Keokuk County, Iowa by about 1850, remaining until about 1870. They then went to Sioux City, Iowa, then to Deadwood, South Dakota and in 1878, to Sturgis.

Upon her death at age 89, the Deadwood, South Dakota *Weekly Pioneer-Times* said that she was likely the oldest woman in the Black Hills and that she was "typical of the pioneer women of the early west. She was of resolute, sturdy old stock, kind of heart and true to her convictions."

Nathaniel and others started the Black Hills Transportation Company, an ox team wagon freight line.

Ephraim Witcher was a member of the Gordon Party of 1874, which intended to find gold in the Black Hills of South Dakota. The party consisted of twenty-eight men, one woman, a ten-year-old boy, six wagons and fifteen yoke of oxen. They left Sioux City, Iowa in the fall of 1874, arriving in the Black Hills on December 23, 1874 after a treacherous twenty-eight-day journey. The woman, Annie D. Tallent, was the first white woman to enter the Black Hills.

They ignored the Fort Laramie Treaty, also known as the Horse

Creek Treaty, that allowed whites passage through Indian land but not settlement, nor mining.

Annie published a book in 1899 entitled, *The Black Hills; Or The Last Hunting Ground of the Dakotahs*, which chronicles their dangerous journey. At one point, Ephraim made the decision to turn back. A council assembled and forbade anyone from leaving the expedition, so he continued on with them. He told Annie, "Well, this is a rather unpleasant experience, but, if you are able to endure the fatigue, the exposure, and all the other disagreeable things of a journey like this, surely, I ought not to complain. I believe if you were not here, we should become totally demoralized."

They built a stockade about two and a half miles below Custer, South Dakota to protect them from attacks by the Lakota Sioux Indians. The walls were of heavy pine timber, thirteen feet in length, set close together in an upright position and three feet in the ground, forming an enclosure of eighty square feet. At each corner were bastions, standing out six feet from the main structure. A large double gate twelve feet wide completed the structure. Inside were seven log cabins, about six feet from the walls of the stockade.

They were successful in finding gold and needed to communicate their discovery to the outside world. Two men, John Gordon, the expedition leader, and Ephraim, volunteered to undertake the journey to Sioux City, Iowa in order to spread the news. As proof of their discovery, they took gold with them, along with supplies, blankets, ammunition and letters from the other expedition members. They set out on February 6, 1875 across untraveled and snow-covered plains.

Mr. Gordon's horse gave out a day out of Yankton, South Dakota and Ephraim went on, arriving in Sioux City twenty-four hours before Mr. Gordon caught up. The news of their discovery soon hit the newspapers.

BLACK HILLS.

Return of Witcher and Gordon from the New Gold Fields.

A Hazardous Homeward March on Account of the Extreme Weather.

They Report the Finding of Gold in the Hills Wherever Prospected For.

The Sioux City Expedition in Good Health and Excellent Spirits.

Figure 77: The Sioux City Journal, *February 28, 1875.*

Back at the stockade, the inhabitants grew weary of waiting for reinforcements to arrive and some left. In April, United States troops arrived to remove those remaining. They were proclaimed prisoners and given twenty-four hours to hunt for their scattered stock and make preparations. They were only allowed to take necessary items of clothing, blankets and provisions. All tools and mining implements were left behind.

The stockade was torn down in 2004 and rebuilt on the original site. It is today a historical landmark located in Custer State Park, South Dakota. The town of Custer is located just west of the stockade.

Figure 78: The Gordon Stockade. *Used with permission of the Custer County Historical Society, 1881 Courthouse Museum.*

Figure 79: Ephraim Witcher, March 1, 1875, on his way from the Black Hills in South Dakota to Sioux City, Iowa. (Tallent, 1899) Image in the public domain.

Ephraim married Clara Etta Boobar and the couple had one daughter, Esther Hollingsworth Witcher, born on March 12, 1882, in Deadwood, South Dakota. The marriage did not last and Clara moved to Minnesota, taking their daughter with her and remarrying in 1888.

In a page from his will written on August 17, 1912, Ephraim wrote that he hadn't heard from his daughter in eight years and that the family believed her to be deceased. He passed away on December 3, 1916 in Chico, California, never knowing what happened to her. Esther was a school teacher in Ohio in 1900, but I have been unsuccessful in locating any additional records.

CHAPTER 15
DESCENDANTS OF GEORGE M. HOLADAY

For the sake of privacy, the following is limited to three generations. For those who are still alive, or if a death date has not been found and it is less than 100 years since their birth, they are listed as "living."

A great deal of effort has gone into ensuring the accuracy of the following, but unfortunately, there are bound to be errors. Please verify and use at your own discretion. Corrections and additional information may be sent to: info@tallgrassprairiebooks.com.

1-**George Meacham Holaday**; born: 8 Oct 1818, Orange Co., IN; died: 5 Sep 1895, Tulare, CA
Mar 1: Lydia Hollingsworth; born: 23 Nov 1819, Union Co., IN; mar: 29 Nov 1838, Vermilion, IL; died: 8 Jul 1911, Winterset, IA
    2-**Samuel Meacham Holaday**; born: 8 Nov 1839, Vermillion Co., IN; died: 29 Mar 1906, Massena, IA; **Mar: Almyra Root**; born: 23 Feb 1841, Crane, OH; mar: 14 Dec 1863, Lewis, IA; died: 31 Oct 1914, Massena, IA

3-**Gertrude Gertie Holaday**; born: 6 May 1866, Winterset, IA; died: 4 Mar 1905, Bonesteel, SD; **Mar: Van James McCurdy**; born: 6 Apr 1856, Dubuque, IA; mar: 1886, Atlantic, IA; died: 26 Dec 1921, Concord, CA

    4-**Ray Elbert McCurdy Sr.**; born: 15 Oct 1888, Massena, IA; mar: Leona Woodgrift; died: 18 Jul 1980, Portland, TN

    4-**Rex Allen McCurdy**; born: 24 Mar 1889, Massena, IA; mar 1: Besse E. Dearmin; mar 2: Esther McCurdy; died: 12 Mar 1976, Silverton, OR

    4-**Sidney S. McCurdy**; born: 22 Jul 1891, Adair Co., IA; died: 23 Feb 1906, Cass Co., IA

    4-**Glenn William McCurdy**; born: 25 Nov 1897, Atlantic, IA; mar: Velma Pauline Sterns; died: 28 Oct 1966, Dunedin, FL

3-**George A. Holaday**; born: 6 Mar 1869, Cass Co., IA; died: 16 Oct 1879, Massena, IA

3-**Charles Abner Holaday**; born: 24 Oct 1870, Massena, IA; died: 14 May 1954, Orient, IA; **Mar 1: Grace Maud Myers**; born: 7 Jun 1875, Winterset, IA.; mar: 6 Jan 1897, Grand River, IA; died: 13 May 1949, IA

    4-**Lloyd Leslie Holaday**; born: 29 Apr 1897, Greenfield, IA; mar: Ruth L. Carey; died: Apr 1976, Colorado Springs, CO

    4-**Benjamin Myron Holaday**; born: 5 Aug 1899, Winterset, Madison, IA; mar: Frances E. Krebs; died: 6 Jun 1979, Winterset, IA

Mar 2: Violet Patton; born: 25 Feb 1883, Lacey, IA; mar: 12 Mar 1907, Fontanelle, IA; died: 3 May 1958, Greenfield, IA

    4-**Almyra Ruth Holaday**; born: 17 Jan 1908, Lee, IA; died: 17 Nov 1930, Creston, IA

    4-**Arthur Stannus Holaday**; born: 22 Apr 1909, Greenfield, IA; mar: Florence Ida Case; died: 6 Sep 2000, Sterling, IL

4-**Sidney Earl Holaday**; born: 12 Oct 1910, Greenfield, IA; mar: Alberta Frances Bart; died: 19 Jul 1997

4-**Gerald Stewart Holaday**; born: 7 May 1913, Greenfield, IA; died: 2 Dec 1943, Lazio, Italy, WWI

4-**Helen Lucile Holaday**; born: 14 Jul 1915, Greenfield, IA; mar: Carl Curtis Malone; died: 2 Feb 2004, Ames, IA

4-**Laurence A. Holaday**; born: 14 Jul 1915, Greenfield, IA; mar: Margaret Alvena Welch; died: 5 Apr 2009, Greenfield, IA

4-**Charles Ernest Holaday**; born: 16 Feb 1920, Greenfield, IA; mar: Jean M. Sears; died: 1 Sep 2000, Greenfield, IA

3-**Thaddeus Samuel Holaday**; born: 12 Mar 1871, Massena, IA; died: 10 Jul 1947, Massena, IA

3-**Myra Lydia Holaday**; born: 7 Jul 1873, Whitneyville, IA; died: 27 Sep 1932, Cumberland, IA; **Mar: John A. Edwards**; born: 4 Feb 1873, IA; mar: 26 Feb 1896, Cumberland, IA; died: 2 Apr 1959, Cumberland, IA

4-**Ruby Gertrude Edwards**; born: 22 Aug 1897, Edna, IA; mar: William Elmer Damon; died: 4 Nov 1977, Safford, AZ

4-**Alice Grethel Edwards**; born: 8 Sep 1899, Edna, IA; mar 1: Hillary Herbert Studley; mar 2: _____ Stotts; died: 16 Dec 1985, Cumberland, IA

4-**Geneva Blanche Edwards**; born: 22 Sep 1906, Cumberland IA; mar: Wilber Gerald South; died: 23 Dec 1990, Polk Co., IA

3-**Roy William Holaday**; born: 9 May 1875, Massena, IA; died: 9 Jun 1937, Massena, IA; **Mar: Minnie Marie Sophia Follmann**; born: 13 May 1879, Bridgewater, IA; mar: 29 Nov 1899, Atlantic, IA; died: 27 Dec 1968, Massena, IA

4-**Amy Marie Holaday**; born: 2 Sep 1900, Massena, IA; mar: Robert Andrew Shaver; died: 7 Jan 1989, Atlantic, IA

4-**Elma Catharine Holaday**; born: 13 Mar 1902, Massena, IA; mar: Earl Harris; died: 22 Nov 1980, Cass Co., IA

4-**Ethel Gertrude Holaday**; born: 13 Aug 1904, Massena, IA; mar: Ernest Harris; died: 28 Jun 1972, Council Bluffs, IA

4-**William Roy Holaday**; born: 3 Apr 1907, Massena, IA; mar: Margaret Elizabeth Jensen; died: 17 Jun 1997, Massena, IA

4-**Charles Arthur Holaday**; born: 9 Aug 1909, Massena, IA; mar: Lela A. Dwigans; died: 30 Aug 1976, Greenfield, IA

4-**Mildred Eva Holaday;** born: 27 Apr 1912, Massena, IA; mar: Royce Hubert Bissell; died: 17 Feb 2005, Fontanelle, IA

4-**Marjorie Lucille Holaday**; born: 4 Mar 1918, Massena, IA; mar 1: Glenn Arthur Shields; mar 2: Francis Marion VanSickle; died: 2 Jan 2001, Fort Collins, CO

3-**Blanche Clara Holaday**; born: 22 Mar 1879, Massena, IA; died: 21 Dec 1955, Greenfield, IA; **Mar: William Follmann**; born: 29 Jul 1877, Bridgewater, IA; mar: 22 Feb 1900; died: 2 Aug 1963, Massena, IA

4-**Gladys C. Follmann**; born: 10 May 1902, IA; mar: Ivan Jensen; died: Apr 1978, Massena, IA

4-**Clarence W. Follman;** born: 12 Nov 1904, Victoria Twp, IA; mar: Mary Wickey; died: Sep 1974, Massena, IA

4-**Clifford Ernest Follmann**; born: 5 Jan 1908, IA; mar: Mildred Yarger; died: 3 Jan 1979, Massena, IA

4-**Ralph Francis Follmann**; born: 21 Feb 1910, Massena, IA; mar: Dolores Lola McKee; died: Jan 1983, Massena, IA

4-**Roy Bernard Follmann**; born: 16 Aug 1912, Massena, IA; mar: Elnora Irene McKee; died: 21 Nov 2000, Atlantic, IA

3-**Harry Miles Holaday**; born: 14 Jan 1881, Whitneyville, IA; died: 17 Jul 1934, Red Oak, IA; **Mar 1: Edna Ethel Matthews**; born: 5 May 1880, Hancock, IL; mar: 6 Nov 1905, Edna Twp., IA; died: 7 Aug 1907, Edna Twp., IA

    4-Glenn M. Holaday; born: 26 Oct 1906, Massena, IA; mar: Verla M. Cheout; died: 20 Aug 1988, Des Moines, IA

Mar 2: Clara Etta Johnson; born: 6 Aug 1883, Cumberland, IA; mar: 16 Dec 1908, Cumberland, IA; died: 9 Jan 1977, San Joaquin, CA

    4-Howard H. Holaday; born: 14 Jan 1912, Massena, IA; mar: Jeanette Lucille Shaw; died: 1 Mar 1968, San Diego, CA

    4-Harold Rex Holaday; born: 6 Jan 1915, Massena, IA; mar: Pearl Ann Johnson; died: 24 Feb 1978, San Diego, CA

3-**Ethel Holaday**; born: 1882, died: 1883 – Massena, IA

3-**Jesse Holaday**; born: 6 Apr 1884, Massena, IA; died: 20 Feb 1962, Massena, IA

2-**Miles Holaday**; born: 20 Mar 1841, Keokuk Co., IA; died: 14 Dec 1916, Tulare, CA; **Mar: Frances J. "Fannie" Mann**; born: 9 May 1854, MO; mar: 16 Jan 1868, Otoe Co., NE; died: 22 Jun 1923, CA

    3-**Virginia "Verdie" L. Holaday**; born: 30 May 1869, NE; died: 6 Oct 1947, Santa Clara, CA; **Mar: Samuel Carter Landram**; born: May 1864, Randolph Co., MO; mar: 31 Dec 1890, Tulare, CA; died: 28 Dec 1932, Los Angeles, CA

        4-Miles Porter Landram; born: 30 Aug 1898, Salinas, CA; mar: Verda L. Gilliam; died: 11 Jul 1946, Los Angeles, CA

    3-**Maude Ann Holaday**; born: 27 Oct 1873, Lincoln, NE; died: 23 Feb 1933, Los Angeles, CA; **Mar 1: James Edward Stockwell Sr.**; born: 14 Dec 1876, IA; mar: Santa Barbara, CA; died: 23 Jul 1948, Orange Co., CA

        4-**Edith Pearl Stockwell**; born: 23 Apr 1901, CA; mar: Charles D. Bradley; died: 10 Jan 1991, Orange Co., CA

        4-**Wallace Edward Stockwell**; born: 22 Mar 1905, Los Angeles City, CA; died: 28 Aug 1917, Newport Beach, CA (drowning accident)

4-**Lois Esther Stockwell**; born: 7 Dec 1907, Los Angeles, CA; died: 15 Sep 1984, Orange Co., CA

4-**John Francis Stockwell Sr.**; born: 11 Sep 1909, Los Angeles, CA; mar: Beatrice M. Capiche; died: 12 Apr 1978, Sacramento, CA

4-**James Edward Stockwell Jr.**; born: 29 Aug 1919, Los Angeles, CA; mar 1: Alice A. Nelson; mar 2: Mildred R. Warren; died: 4 Jan 1970, Santa Barbara, CA

Mar 2: William L. Cochran; born: 3 Dec 1870, IA; mar: 1892; died: 4 Sep 1944, San Mateo Co., CA

3-**James Manton Holaday**; born: 12 Sep 1875, NE; died: 28 Apr 1933, Madera, CA

3-**Nathan Andrew Holaday**; born: 7 May 1878, Stockton, CA; died: 14 May 1947, Monterey, CA; **Mar: Mae Belle Chase**; born: 28 Apr 1884, NY; died: 2 Dec 1977, Salinas, CA

4-**Alfred Chase Holaday**; born: 22 Apr 1910, Salinas, CA; mar: Janie Pepper McWillie; died: 15 May 1979, San Francisco, CA

4-**Thais Jean Holaday**; born: 16 Dec 1913, Salinas, CA; mar 1: Louis William Salmina; mar 2: Richard Charles Attinger; died: 7 Sep 1993, Salinas, CA

4-**Miles Eugene Holaday**; born: 5 Jun 1917, Salinas, CA; mar 1: Sarah Paisley Mulock; mar 2: Marie Teresa Hartnell; died: 14 Nov 2003, Salinas, CA

3-**George Frederic Holaday**; born: 29 Jan 1881, Stockton, CA; died: 7 Jan 1960, Tulare, CA; **Mar: Irene Carpenter**; born: 29 Mar 1883, CA; mar: 4 Jan 1904, Tulare, CA; died: 27 Apr 1956, Tulare, CA

4-**Kenneth Leo Holaday, Judge**; born: 25 Dec 1904, Tulare, CA; mar: Neva D. Abshire; died: 22 Apr 1980, Burbank, CA

4-**Leroy C. Holaday**; born: 27 Nov 1910, Tulare Co, CA; mar: Lorraine F. Johnson; died: 14 Oct 1974, Exeter, CA

3-**Benjamin Franklin Holaday**; born: 14 Feb 1883, Tulare, CA; died: 16 Aug 1967, Los Angeles, CA; **Mar: Grace Belle Corey**; born: abt 1897, WA; mar: 28 Jun 1913, Los Angeles, CA; died: 28 May 1934, Alameda, CA
    4-**Infant son**; born: 1915; died: 1915
    4-**Jacquelyn May Holaday**; born: 28 Oct 1926, Alameda, CA; mar 1: Neely Overland Hoopiiaina; mar 2: Vernon Robert Hillger; died: 13 Nov 2012

3-**Frances Pearl Holaday**; born: May 1885, CA; died: 16 Oct 1912, Los Angeles Co., CA; **Mar: Charles A Helbach**; born: abt 1884, WI; mar: 25 Apr 1908, Santa Ana, CA; died: unk

3-**Wallace Earl Holaday**; born: 19 Mar 1888, Tulare, CA; died: 27 Apr 1960, Bakersfield, CA; **Mar: Gladys Martha Thomson**; born: 4 Oct 1887, CA; mar: abt 1911; died: 10 Jul 1977, Bakersfield, CA
    4-**William Thomson Holaday**; born: 25 Dec 1912, Tulare, CA; mar: Elizabeth Jean Jenkins; died: 25 Aug 1985, Kern Co., CA
    4-**Gayle B. Holaday**; born: 3 Apr 1917, Tulare, CA, mar: William Berry Pyles, Jr.; died: 4 Jul 1971, Los Angeles, CA

3-**Carter Miles Holaday**; born: 23 Mar 1891, Tulare, CA; died: 11 Dec 1928, Tulare, CA; **Mar: Irene P. "Rena" Poore**; born: 30 Sep 1896, CA; mar: 23 Dec 1916, Fresno, CA; died: 7 Oct 1984, Fresno, CA
    4-**Phyllis Layne Holaday**; born: 19 Sep 1917, Fresno, CA; mar: Frank W. Saul; died: 21 Oct 1986, Santa Clara, CA
    4-**Lorraine Holaday**; born: 18 Aug 1919, CA; died: 14 Jun 1974, Fresno, CA

2-**John Milton Holaday**; born: Sep 1842, Richland, IA; died: 3 Jan 1926, Colorado Springs, CO; **Mar: Mary Kinman**; born: 1854, OH; mar: abt 1871; died: 5 Feb 1928, CO
    3-**Will Tipton Holaday**; born: 11 Feb 1872, IA; died: 27 Oct 1876, Council Bluffs, IA

3-**Florence C. Holaday**; born: 14 Apr 1877, Omaha, NE; died: 29 Feb 1960, Denver, CO; **Mar: Robert Valentine Weicker**; born: 9 Dec 1864, Carroll Co., MO; mar: 7 Aug 1895, Denver, CO; died: 20 Dec 1949, Denver, CO

> 4-**Irma Mary Weicker**; born: 14 Jun 1903, Denver, CO; mar: Robert Van Horn Work; died: 28 Mar 1970, Denver, CO
>
> 4-**Eunice Elizabeth Weicker**; born: 17 Jul 1906, Denver, CO; died: 27 Jan 1930, Biloxi, MS

2-**Caroline Holaday**; born: 27 Nov 1844, Keokuk Co., IA; died: 11 Sep 1930, Los Angeles, CA; **Mar: Benjamin Franklin "Frank" Murray, Senator**; born: 20 Aug 1838, OH; mar: 8 Nov 1864, Winterset, IA; died: 7 May 1890, Winterset, IA

> 3-**Lenore Kate Murray**; born: 13 Sep 1865, Winterset, IA; died: 22 Dec 1951, Los Angeles, CA; **Mar: Emerson Bond Weirick**; born: July 1855, PA; mar: 17 Nov 1892, Winterset, IA; died: 1 Oct 1925, Portland, OR
>
>> 4-**Arthur Murray Weirick**; born: 16 Oct 1893, Helena, MT; mar: Margaret Mae Lowry; died: 18 May 1972, Corona, CA
>>
>> 4-**Maud Helen Weirick**; born: 10 Dec 1895, Silver Bow Co., MT; mar: Parker Vorhees Foster, Sr.; died: 6 Mar 1990, San Diego, CA
>>
>> 4-**Josephine Frances Weirick**; born: 26 Dec 1901, Butte, MT; mar: Robert Lenox Banks; died: 15 Sep 1967, Marshfield, WI
>
> 3-**Thaddeus S. Murray;** born: 2 Jun 1866, Winterset, IA; died: 18 Feb 1869, Winterset, IA
>
> 3-**Maude Murray**; born: 21 Apr 1868, Winterset, IA; died: 5 Aug 1952, Los Angeles, CA; **Mar 1: Thomas F. Ward**; born: abt 1862, IA or PA; mar: 12 Sep 1895, Great Falls, MT; died: 1917–1919

4-**Murray A Ward**; born: 7 Apr 1901, Le Mars, IA; mar: Virginia Leonide Ducommun; died: 17 Jan 1985, Beverly Hills, CA

Mar 2: Daniel Moore Locey; born: 14 Aug 1879, St Louis, MO; mar: 10 Feb 1916, Phoenix, AZ; died: 23 Jul 1935, Cleveland, OH

3-**Nicholas William Murray**; born: 7 Mar 1871, Winterset, IA; died: 17 Feb 1929, Los Angeles, CA; **Mar: Josephine Claudine Dupin**; born: 14 Feb 1872, New Orleans, LA; mar: 1906; died: 27 Jun 1944, Birmingham, AL

4-**Frank Blair Murray Sr.**; born: 24 Mar 1907, Orleans, LA; mar: Emma Arnette Price; died: 14 Feb 1996, Birmingham, AL

3-**Elizabeth "Bessie" Murray**; born: 30 Jul 1876, Winterset, IA; died: 30 Jul 1956, Los Angeles, CA; **Mar 1: Charles James Newman**; born: 15 Dec 1872, Denver, CO; mar: 25 Dec 1902, Oakland, CA; died: 28 Feb 1959, Santa Rosa, CA.

Mar 2: Frank Wiley Shepherd; born: 28 Feb 1876, Dundee Twp, IL.; mar: 20 Dec 1913, Cook, IL; died: 18 Oct 1945, Elgin, IL

4-**Carolyn Virginia Shepherd**; born: 5 Nov 1914, Elgin, IL.; mar: Kenneth Vernon McCullough; died: 8 May 2016, Somerville, NJ

2-**Emma Caroline Holaday**; born: 16 Aug 1846, Sigourney, IA; died: 26 Mar 1918, Greenfield, IA; **Mar: Royal Oran Brown**; born: May 1846, Freedom, OH; mar: 6 Feb 1868, Adair, IA; died: 4 Jun 1919, Greenfield, IA

3-**Cora Belle Brown**; died at birth or young, dates unknown

3-**Frederick Royal Brown**; born: 8 Mar 1869, Orient, IA; died: 22 Dec 1967, Clinton, OK; **Mar: Mina Maye Bevington**; born: 28 Feb 1878, Nashville, Ohio; mar: 25 Dec 1893, Adair Co., IA; died: 12 Feb 1960, Clinton, OK

4-**Georgia Ailena Brown**; born: 28 Jan 1895, Orient, IA; mar: Thomas August Raasch, Sr.; died: 5 Nov 1967, Hobart, OK

>   4-**Cleo Cecilia Brown**; born: 21 Jul 1896, Orient, IA; mar 1: Joe Ogle; mar 2: Joe King; died: 14 Jan 1979, Clinton, OK
>
>   4-**Nora Estelle Brown**; born: 12 Aug 1899, Bessie, OK; mar: Orville R. Eaton; died: 19 Apr 1986, Washington, WI
>
>   4-**Opal Roberta Brown**; born: 2 Dec 1899, Bessie, OK; mar: Grady B. Watson; died: 1996
>
>   4-**Cecil Alvin Brown**; born: 14 Jan 1904, Bessie, OK; died: 23 Jan 1904, Bessie, OK
>
>   4-**Royal Owen Brown**; born: 2 Sep 1908, Greenfield, IA; mar: Bess Arlene _____; died: 21 Sep 1983, La Habra, CA
>
>   4-**Mina Maye Brown**; born: 16 Feb 1919, OK; mar: John H. Turley; died: 6 Aug 1994, Humboldt, CA

3-**Nellie M. Brown**; born: 14 Jan 1871, Fontanelle, IA; died: 8 May 1895; **Mar: George H. Schnellbacher**; born: Adair Co., IA; mar: 10 Jul 1894, Adair Co., IA

3-**Edward Roscoe Brown**; born: 11 Nov 1876, Greenfield, IA; died: 1 Nov 1952, Des Moines, IA; **Mar: Katherine Cowell**, born: abt 1873, Manchester IA; mar: 2 May 1900, Delaware, IA; died: 14 Dec 1961

3-**Allie Maude Brown**; born: 1878, IA; died: Adair Co., IA

3-**Robert Burns Brown**; born: 15 Mar 1880, Greenfield, IA; died: 19 Oct 1943, Arispe, IA; **Mar: Cora Edna Bevington**; born: 22 Nov 1883, Hanover, OH; mar: 15 Mar 1904, Hebron, IA; died: Apr 1972, Chariton, IA

>   4-**Margorie Brown**; born: 26 Oct 1906, Union Twp, Adair Co., IA; mar: Elmer R. Burch; died: 20 Jan 1985, Los Angeles, CA

3-**Harry Garfield Brown**; born: 25 Jan 1886, Hebron, IA; died: 1961; **Mar: Flora Helena Putzier**; born: abt 1887, Eagle Grove, IA; mar: 4 Feb 1910, Bancroft, IA; died: 1977

>   4-**Gerald Oran Brown**; born: 27 Nov 1911, IA; died: 24 Mar 1987, Des Moines, IA

3-**Jay Eugene Brown**; born: 22 Mar 1889, Greenfield, IA; died: 22 Oct 1951, Des Moines, IA; **Mar: Carrie Fay Pooler**; born: 25 Apr 1891, Hebron, IA; mar: 21 Apr 1908, Adair Co., IA; died: 12 Jan 1943, Creston, IA
    4-**Donald Eugene Brown**; born: 12 Feb 1910, IA; mar: Verdie Valeria Sachau; died: 17 Feb 1958, Lubbock, TX
    4-**Harold Forest Brown**; born: 14 Feb 1912, Union Twp, Adair Co., IA; mar: Doris Leona Lake; died: 25 Oct 1986, Creston, IA
3-**Allan R. Brown**; born: 18 Nov 1892, Greenfield, IA; died: 20 Apr 1961, Greenfield, IA; **Mar: Emma L. Zellweger**; born: 22 Mar 1893, Greenfield, IA; mar: 29 Oct 1911, Hill of Zion, Adair Co., IA; died: 21 Jul 1982, Greenfield, IA
    4-**Gertrude Helen Brown**; born: 5 Sep 1912, Orient, IA; mar: Orlie James Sheriff; died: 6 Sep 2006, Greenfield, IA
    4-**Kenneth A. Brown**; born: 13 Jan 1914, IA; mar: Mandale J. Henderson; died: 30 Aug 1976, Shasta, CA
    4-**Solan Sylvester Brown**; born: 13 Mar 1916, Greenfield, IA; mar: Edith Rizzi; died: 29 Feb 1992, Shasta, CA
2-**Ellen Holaday**; born: 16 Aug 1846, Sigourney, IA; died: abt 1891, Denison, TX; **Mar 1: John Gallagher**; born: abt 1840; mar: 10 Feb 1882, Sherman, TX; **Mar 2:** P. Bradley, mar: 25 Nov 1889, Sherman, TX
2-**William Holaday**; born: 25 Mar 1848, Keokuk Co., IA; died: 26 Nov 1931, Greenfield, IA; **Mar: Jennett Anna Gaylord**; born: Aug 1849, IA; mar: 16 Jul 1873, Montgomery, IA; died: 9 Mar 1926, Greenfield, IA
    3-**Cleo A. Holaday**; born: 23 Jun 1874, Cass Co., IA; died: 4 Jul 1964, Quincy, IL; **Mar: James Thomas Taylor**; born: 15 Nov 1872, Polk Co., IA; mar: 25 Nov 1893, Greenfield, IA; died 15 Dec 1953, Cedar Rapids, IA

4-**Helen Maurine Taylor**; born: 11 Feb 1896, Greenfield, IA; mar 1: Howard Funk; mar 2: Howard Tipton Fuller; died: 31 May 1964, Quincy, IL

4-**Marjory Louise Taylor**; born: 24 Sep 1902, Greenfield, IA; mar: Leo Letoire Burrell; died: 11 Dec 1988, Madison, WI

3-**Clarance Holaday***; born: 2 Nov 1875, Greenfield, IA; died: 13 Oct 1953, Fort Harrison, MT; **Mar: Bessie L. Wilkinson**; born: 29 Nov 1878, Webster Co., IA; died: 6 Dec 1972, Libby, MT

4-**William Holiday**, Rev.; born: 9 Apr 1910, Irving, KS; mar: Elsa L. Slaughter; died: 6 Dec 1967, Ontario, OR

4-**Robert Samuel Holiday**; born: 29 Feb 1912, Alberta, Canada; mar: Amy Riley; died: 18 Jan 1997, Libby, MT

4-**Edward Sidney Holiday**; born: 7 Sep 1916, Alberta, Canada; mar: Margaret A. Huchala; died: 14 May 1996, Libby, MT

4-**Ruth Margaret Holiday**; born: 10 Jan 1921, Irving, KS; mar: Paul Pitcher; died: 18 Oct 2006, Knoxville, TN

3-**Ethel Edna Holaday**; born: 2 Mar 1879, Cass Co., IA; died: 1957, Des Moines, IA; **Mar: George E. Cromley**; born: 30 Jan 1882, Cass Co., IA; mar: 5 Jun 1909, Des Moines, IA; died: 4 Mar 1937, Des Moines, IA

3-**Dora Holaday**; born: Feb 1881, Cass Co., IA; died: 1920, Des Moines, IA; **Mar: Roy Merriam Fletcher**; born: 1 Jul 1874, Brookfield, MO; mar: May 1913, Des Moines, IA; died: 25 Apr 1954, Los Angeles, CA

2-**Thomas Jefferson Holaday**; born: 1854, Jefferson Twp, IA; died: 1855, Jefferson Twp, IA

2-**Orpha Holaday**; born: 1856, Adair Co., IA; died: bef 1860, Adair or Madison Co., IA

2-**Pauline Holaday**; born: 19 Jun 1857, Des Moines, IA; died: 9 Apr 1936, Oakland, CA; **Mar: Albert Rush Dabney**; born: 7 Feb 1845, Vermilion, IL; mar: 19 Jun 1877, Winterset, IA; died: 13 Jun 1913, Oakland, CA

3-**Clara Bell Dabney**; born: 19 Feb 1878, Winterset, IA; died: 30 Jun 1960, Alameda, CA

3-**Lenore Pauline Dabney**; born: 7 Aug 1880, Winterset, IA; died: 29 Jan 1975, Alameda, CA; **Mar 1: William Frederick Schwaner Sr.**; born: 13 Jan 1873, Winterset, IA; mar: 28 Sep 1900, Winterset, IA; died: 23 Apr 1927, Oakland, CA

    4-**Albert Dabney Schwaner**; born: 18 Sep 1901, Oakland, CA; mar: Jasmine Violet Ball; died: 21 Jul 1980, Oakland, CA

    4-**William Frederick Schwaner Jr.**; born: 18 Jun 1906, Oakland, CA; died: 9 Feb 1924, Oakland, CA

    4-**John Edward Schwaner**; born: 12 Oct 1908, CA; mar: Joyce L. Rowe; died: 6 Sep 1983, Sacramento, CA

  Mar 2: Albert B. Saurman; born: abt 1870, PA; mar: abt 1930

3-**Alice M. Dabney**; born: 20 Apr 1885, IA; died: 30 Dec 1975, Oakland, CA; **Mar: Julius Carl Seulberger**; born: 7 Oct 1884, CA; mar: 28 Apr 1909, Alameda, CA; died: 28 Apr 1978, Oakland, CA

    4-**Alice Pauline Seulberger**; born: 9 Jun 1914, Alameda, CA; mar: Robert Fielding Johnson; died: unk

    4-**Barbara Jane Seulberger**; born: 23 Sep 1921, Oakland, CA; mar: Evan Townsend Pugh; died: 19 Jul 2007

3-**Helen Jane Dabney**; born: 4 Aug 1891, Winterset, IA; died: 27 Sep 1982, Alameda, CA; **Mar 1: Thomas Patrick Hogan Jr.**; born: 13 Oct 1891, Oakland, CA; mar: 1913, CA; died: 12 Jul 1941, Alameda, CA

    4-**Thomas Patrick Hogan III**; born: 27 May 1916, Alameda, CA; mar: Mary Francis Orrick; died: 17 Oct 1984, Berkeley, CA

    4-**Albert Dabney Hogan**; born: 2 Jan 1919, Alameda, CA; mar: Jeanne Valerie Guittard; died: 31 Dec 1966, Alameda, CA

4-**Robert Hogan**; born: 11 Jan 1921, Alameda, CA; died: 13 Mar 1972, Redding, CA

Mar 2: John F. Sheehy; born: 23 Jan 1895, Watsonville, CA; mar: 28 Mar 1951, Alameda, CA; died: 27 Jun 1977, Alameda, CA

2-**Henry Delano Holaday**; born: 10 Apr 1860, Winterset, IA; died: 28 Nov 1924, Massena, IA; **Mar: Mary M. Spies**; born: 10 Mar 1864, Shannon, IL; mar: 10 May 1885, Franklin Twp, IA; died: Jun 1963, Massena, IA

3-**Louisa Bessie Holaday**; born: 1 Jan 1886, Denison, TX; died: 28 Apr 1968, Winters, CA; **Mar: William Spies**; born: 5 Oct 1877, Bennington, IA; mar: 27 Jun 1912, Massena, IA; died: 22 Apr 1944, Contra Costa, CA

4-**Mary Averil Spies**; born: 23 Sep 1913, Ziebach, SD; mar 1: Leonard Lee Barkhousen; mar 2: Harold H. Slocum; died: 7 Sep 1994, Turlock, CA

4-**Varel Everett Spies**; born: 7 Oct 1916, Massena, IA; died: 9 Feb 1985, Turlock, CA

4-**Lorraine Deloris Spies**; born: 22 Sep 1920, Massena, IA; mar: Charles Frank Holbrook; died: 14 Jun 1986, Montrose, PA

3-**George Spies Holaday**; born: 29 Jun 1893, Massena, IA; died: Dec 1979, Massena, IA; **Mar: Gladys Bell McBride**; born: 17 Dec 1893, Union, IA; mar: 1912, IA; died: 10 Sep 1975, Massena, IA

4-**Helen Bell Holaday**; born: 19 Oct 1927, Atlantic, IA; mar: Levern V. Petersen, Council Bluffs, IA; died: 9 Jan 2004, Council Bluffs, IA

4-**Marilyn Ruth Holaday**; born: 9 Mar 1930, Atlantic, IA; died: before 27 Mar 2023

4-**Mary Joan Holaday**; born: 24 Nov 1934, Atlantic, IA; mar: Alvin Francis Streb; died: 27 Mar 2023, Iowa City, IA

3-**Gladys Merle Holaday**; born: 7 May 1900, Victoria, IA; died: 24 Nov 1991; **Mar: Joseph John Holste**; born: 4 Mar 1900, Massena, IA; mar: 2 Dec 1920, Creston, IA; died: 26 Sep 1980, Atlantic, IA

    4-**living**; mar: living

    4-**Berniece Eleanor Holste**; born: 30 Dec 1925, Victoria, IA; mar Ernest Arkle Thompson; died: 25 Apr 2004, Des Moines, IA

3-**Clifford Arthur Holaday**; born: 26 Dec 1902, Massena, IA; died: Dec 1972, Anita, IA; **Mar: Reba Catherine King**; born: 17 Jun 1907, Anita, IA; mar: 10 Apr 1926, Atlantic, IA; died: 12 Dec 2000, Atlantic, IA

    4-**Byron C. Holaday**; born: 13 Jan 1927, Massena, IA; died: 14 Jan 1927, Massena, IA

    4-**Dorothy Irene Holaday**; born: 13 Jan 1928, Massena, IA; mar: Dallas Bennesen; died: 22 Feb 2010, Atlantic, IA

    4-**Wayland Gail Holaday**; born: 12 Aug 1929, Massena, IA; mar: Patsy Ann Lanteri; died: 15 May 1996, Anita, IA

    4-**Henry George "Hank" Holaday**; born: 2 Sep 1931, Massena, IA; mar: living; died: 30 Sep 2018, Anita, IA

    4-**Grover Varel Holaday**; born: 3 Jul 1933, Massena, IA; mar: living; died: 10 Dec 2019, Atlantic, IA

    4-**Marjorie Marie Holaday**; born: 8 Jan 1935, IA; mar: Richard William Eblen; died: 27 Oct 2007, Panora, IA

    4-**Ruth Elaine Holaday**; born: 29 Apr 1941, Massena, IA; mar: Leo D. Hellyer; died: 28 Nov 2022, Des Moines, IA

    4-**Clifford Gary Holaday**; born: 13 Mar 1944; mar: living; died: 1 Aug 2001, Morris Co., KS

Mar 2: Elvira (Collins?); born: 1829, OH or NY; died: 5 Jul 1864, La Paz, AZ

2-**George Washington Holaday**; born: 2 Mar 1859, IA; died: 19 Jan 1926, San Diego, CA; **Mar: Sarah Isabel Atwood**; born: 2 Mar 1867, San Bernardino, CA; mar: San Bernardino, CA; died: 26 Aug 1954, Whittier, CA

    3-**Clarence Weinwright Holaday**; born: 7 Jan 1885, CA; died: 31 Jul 1951, Humboldt, CA; **Mar: Bessie M** _____; born: abt 1894, IA

    3-**Ethel Elvira Holaday**; born: 28 Nov 1887, CA; died: 25 Nov 1980, Whittier, CA; **Mar: Elmer John "Frank" Van Horn**; born: 10 Jul 1878, Hanford, CA; mar: 19 Dec 1905, San Bernardino, CA; died: 10 Dec 1962, Riverside, CA

        4-**Melba Minnie Van Horn**; born: 21 Apr 1913, San Diego, CA; mar: Lorenze Frank Cox; died: 13 Dec 2001, Chino Hills, CA

    3-**Leo William Holaday**; born: 13 May 1889, San Bernardino, CA; died: 24 Apr 1953, San Diego, CA

    3-**Eva M Holaday**; born: Oct 1894, CA; died: 25 Dec 1938, San Diego, CA; **Mar: Walter Deo McCool**; born: 8 Aug 1888, San Diego, CA; mar: 28 Apr 1914, Los Angeles, CA; died: 20 Oct 1966, Alameda, CA

2-**Arizona Holaday**; born: Apr 1864, La Paz, AZ; died: unknown
Mar 3: Mary E. Robinson; born: 1833, TN; mar: 1868, San Francisco, CA; died: unknown

---

*Clarence Holaday/Holiday: Born with the surname of "Holaday," he changed it to "Holiday." His descendants bear the latter name. Clarence's entry in the index is under the name he was born with; ie, Holaday.

REFERENCES

Acts, Resolutions and Memorials, Adopted by the First Legislative Assembly of the Territory of Arizona. (1865). Prescott, Arizona, USA: Office of the Arizona Miner.

An Illustrated History of Southern Caifornia. (1890). Chicago, IL, USA: The Lewis Publishing Company.

> Note: Excerpts from this book were paraphrased in Chapter 4. George M. Holaday's biography that appears in *An Illustrated History* is printed in its entirety in Chapter 11, Death of a Pioneer, with added paragraph breaks.

Bieber, Ralph P. (1927, December). Diary of a Journey to the Pike's Peak Gold Mines in 1859. *The Mississippi Valley Historical Review, 14*(3).

Boaz, A. (2024, June 23). *Individuals in this page: Robert Holaday & Edith Davis.* Retrieved 2024, from Specific Ancestral Lines of the Boaz, Paul, Welty & Fishel Families: https://www.specificancestrallines.com/robert-holiday-and-edith-davis.html

Boaz, A. (2024, June 23). *Individuals in this page: William Holaday & Jane Andrew.* Retrieved 2024, from Specific Ancestral Lines of the Boaz, Paul, Welty & Fishel Families: https://www.specificancestrallines.com/william-holaday-and-jane-andrew.html

Bresee, Floyd E. (1937). *Overland Freighting in the Platte Valley 1850-1870.* Thesis, University of Nebraska, Lincoln.

Carter, C. E. (1939). *The Territorial Papers of the United States* (Vol. VII). (C. E. Carter, Ed.) Washington, D.C., USA: U.S. Gov't

Continental Historical Company. (1884). *History of Cass County, Iowa; together with sketches of its towns, villages, and townships; educational, civil, military, and political history; portraits of prominent persons, and biographies of old settlers and representative citizens. History of Iowa,.* Springfield, IL, USA: Continental Historical Company.

Courtney, B. G. (2015). *Prescott's Original Whiskey Row.* USA: The History Press.

References

Florin, Lambert (1967). *A Guide to Western Ghost Towns*. Seattle, USA: Superior Publishing Company.

Friends in Illiana 1826; Abstracts of the Records of the Society of Friends of Vermilion Quarterly Meeting in Vermilion Grove, Illinois. (1970). Danville, IL, USA: Illiana Genealogical & Historical Society.

Galland, Isaac (1840). *Galland's Iowa Emigrant: Containing a Map and General Descriptions of Iowa Territory*. Chillicothe [O.] : W. C. Jones.

Ganavj, Kathad (2015). *Hualapai*. Retrieved from Hualapai: https://hualapai-nsn.gov/wp-content/uploads/2015/03/KathadGanavjlapazstory.pdf

Hamilton, Patrick. (1883). *The Resources of Arizona : a description of its mineral, farming, grazing and timber lands; its rivers, mountains, valleys and plains; its cities, towns and mining camps; its climate and productions; with brief sketches of its early history, pre-historic.* (2, Ed.) San Francisco, CA, USA: A.L. Bancroft & Co, Printers.

History of Lawrence, Orange and Washington Counties Indiana: From the Earliest Time to the Present, Together with Interesting Biographical Sketches, Reminiscences, Notes, Etc. (1884). Chicago, IL, USA: Godspeed Bros & Co.

Hollingsworth, Douglas. (2013, April 22). *Hollingsworth Family Origins*. Retrieved from Valentine Hollingsworth: https://www.valentinehollingsworth.com/

Hussey, Tacitus (1919). *Beginnings; Reminiscences of Early Des Moines*. Des Moines, IA, USA: American Lithographing and Ptg. Co.

Jones, Louis E. (1911). *History Of Vermilion County Illinois; A Tale of its Evolution, Settlement and Progress For Nearly A Century* (Vol. I). Chicago, IL: Pioneer Publishing Company.

Jones, Louis T. (1911). *Salem, the Pioneer Quaker Community of Iowa*. University of Kansas. Lawrence, KS: KU ScholarWorks.

Jones, Louis T. (1914). *The Quakers of Iowa*. State University of Iowa, Iowa City.

Kilburn, Lucian M. (1915). *History of Adair County, Iowa, and its People* (Vol. I). Chicago, IL, USA: The Pioneer Publishing Company.

References

Lowe, Col W.W. (1885). *Dr. Enos Lowe*. University of Nebraska - Lincoln. Lincoln: Nebraska State Historical Society.

MacHunter, Aundrey, & Henderson, Randall. (1958, September). Boom Days in Old La Paz. *Desert Magazine*.

Mueller, Herman A. (Ed.). (1915). *History of Madison County Iowa and its People* (Vol. I). Chicago, IL, USA: The S.J. Clarke Publishing Company.

Munson, E. S. (n.d.). Looking at History: Indiana's Hoosier National Forest Region, 1600 to 1950. United States Forest Service. Retrieved from http://npshistory.com/publications/usfs/region/9/hoosier/history.pdf

Murray, Caroline (1908, March 17). *Life in Madison County During the Civil War*. Retrieved from IaGenWeb: https://iagenweb.org/madison/military/american_civil_war/life_during_war.html

Note: Caroline speaks of her husband Benjamin Franklin "Frank," being imprisoned at Andersonville, South Carolina. Per Frank's Civil War records, he was actually imprisoned in three prisons; the last one at Montgomery, Alabama, but never at Andersonville.

Northern Arizona University, Cline Library. (2005). *Indigenous Voices of the Colorado Plateau*. Retrieved from Northern Arizona University, Cline Library Special Collections: https://library.nau.edu/speccoll/exhibits/indigenous_voices/hualapai/events.html

Petersen, William J. (1963). The Geography of Iowa Territory. *The Palimpsest, 44*(6).

Reid, Teanu (2016, April 7-9). *Road Through a Home: A History of the Bush River Quaker Settlement in Colonial South Carolina*. Retrieved 2024, from NCUR Proceedings.

Renner, Pamela (1974). La Paz - Gateway to Territorial Arizona. *The Journal of Arizona History, 24*(2), 119-144.

Russell, Hubert D. (1906). *The Complete Story of the San Francisco Horror by the Survivors and Rescuers*. San Francisco: unknown.

Sabin, Henry S. & Edward L. (1900). *The Making of Iowa* (Fourth ed.). Chicago, IL: A. Flanagan Co.

References

Summerhayes, Martha (1911). *Vanished Arizona Recollections of the Army Life of a New England Woman* (2 ed.). Salem, Massachusetts, USA: The Salem Press.

Tallent, Annie D. (1899). *The Black Hills; Or, The Last Hunting Ground of the Dakotahs*. St. Louis, MO, USA: Nixon-Jones Printing Company.

Note: The description of the stockade in Ephraim Witcher's Mini Biography in Chapter 14 is from Annie Tallent's book. The narrative of Ephraim's Gordon Party of 1874 experience is paraphrased from the same.

The History of Keokuk County, Iowa, Containing a History of the County, its Cities, Towns &c.,. (1880). Des Moines, IA: The Union Historical Company.

The History of Madison County, Iowa, Containing A History of the County, its Cities, Towns, Etc. (1879). Des Moines, IA, USA: Union Historical Company.

The History and Future of Dos Palmas. University of California Riverside Palm Desert Center. (2021, January 2021).

Tour of Iowa Counties, Adair County. (1868, November 18). Daily State Register, VII (275).

United States Forest Service. (n.d.). *Lick Creek African American Settlement*. Retrieved from United States Forest Service: https://www.fs.usda.gov/detail/hoosier/specialplaces/?cid=fsbdev3_017495

Waite, John C. (1970). *An Annotated Subject Bibliography of the Acts, Resolutions, and Memorials of the Arizona Territorial Legislatures from 1864 to 1899*. The University of Arizona.

Wikipedia Contributors. (2024, June 13). *George Washington Carver*. (Wikipedia, The Free Encyclopedia) Retrieved from Wikipedia: https://en.wikipedia.org/w/index.php?title=George_Washington_Carver&oldid=1228810770

Wikipedia Contributors. (2023, May 17). *Rancho Larkin's Children*. (Wikipedia, The Free Encyclopedia) Retrieved from Wikipedia: https://en.wikipedia.org/w/index.php?title=Rancho_Larkin%27s_Children&oldid=1155349897

Woody, Clara T. (1962). The Woolsey Expeditions of 1864. *Arizona and the West, 4*(2), 157-176.

INDEX

A

Abshire, Neva D. · 196
Adair County, Iowa · 70
Agnews State Hospital · 139
Alcorn, William · 71
Alderson Women's Prison · 181
Amos, Catherine · 146
Amos, William · 146
Apache Indians · 109
Arizona Territory · 96
Attinger, Richard Charles · 196
Atwood, Danford · 173
Atwood, Jane · 173
Atwood, Sarah Isabel · 173, 174, 206

B

Bagley, Ezekiel · 146
Bagley, Horace Newton · 146
Bagley, Horace Newton Jr. · 177
Bagley, Horace Newton Sr. · 146, 177
Bagley, Jerusha Jane · 146, 177
Bagley, John · 146
Bagley, John E. · 146
Bagley, John Ezekiel · 177
Bagley, Mary Amelia · 146, 177
Bagley, Tryphena Ann · 146, 177
Bakersfield, California · 132
Ball, Jasmine Violet · 203
Banks, Robert Lenox · 198
Barkhousen, Leonard Lee · 204
Barnett, Margaret · 146
Bart, Alberta Frances · 192
Battle of Pea Ridge, Arkansas · 93, 155
Battle of Shiloh, Tennessee · 159
Beauchamp, John W. · 108
Bennesen, Dallas · 205
Bevington, Cora Edna · 200
Bevington, Mina Maye · 199
Birdcage Saloon · 122

Bishop, Clarissa · 27
Bissell, Royce Hubert · 194
Black Hills Transportation Company · 186
Black, Reuben · 25
Boobar, Clara Etta · 189
Bradley, Charles D. · 195
Bradley, P. · 167
Bradshaw Road · 98
Bradshaw Trail · 99
Bradshaw, William D. · 98
Brians, George Washington · 125
Brown, Allan R. · 201
Brown, Allie Maude · 200
Brown, Cecil Alvin · 200
Brown, Cleo Cecilia · 200
Brown, Cora Belle · 199
Brown, Donald Eugene · 201
Brown, Edward Roscoe · 200
Brown, Frederick Royal · 199
Brown, Georgia Ailena · 199
Brown, Gerald Oran · 200
Brown, Gertrude H. · 201
Brown, Harold Forest · 201
Brown, Harry Garfield · 200
Brown, Jay Eugene · 201
Brown, Kenneth A. · 201
Brown, Margorie · 200
Brown, Mina Maye · 200
Brown, Nellie M. · 200
Brown, Nora Estella · 200
Brown, Opal Roberta · 200
Brown, Robert Burns · 200
Brown, Royal Oran · 127, 165, 199
Brown, Royal Owen · 200
Brown, Solan Sylvester · 201
Burch, Elmer R. · 200
Burrell, Leo Letoire · 202
Burroughs, Jerusha · 146
Bush River Monthly Meeting · 19
Bush River, South Carolina · 18, 22

Index

C

California Trail · 54
Capiche, Beatrice M. · 196
Carey, Ruth L. · 192
Carolina Colony · 22
Carpenter, Irene · 196
Carver, George Washington · 81
Case, Florence Ida · 192
Cass County Gazette · 155
Cass County, Iowa · 93, 150
Chase, Mae Belle · 196
Chatham, North Carolina · 17
Cheout, Verla M. · 195
Civil War · 93, 102, 169
Clarinda Insane Asylum · 161
Cochran, William L. · 196
Coffin, Lorenzo S. · 181
Collins, Elvira · 74, 76, 85, 92, 95, 102, 138, 205
Colusa, California · 60, 63
Corey, Grace B. · 196
Council Bluffs, Iowa · 67
Cowell, Katherine · 200
Cox, Lorenze Frank · 206
Cromley, George E. · 202
Crow, Elizabeth · 71
Custer, South Dakota · 187

D

Dabney, Albert Rush · 128, 168, 202
Dabney, Alice M. · 203
Dabney, Clara Bell · 203
Dabney, Helen Jane · 170, 203
Dabney, Lenore Pauline · 203
Damon, William Elmer · 193
Danville, Illinois · 24
Dearborn County, IN · 22
Dearmin, Besse E. · 192
Des Moines, Polk County, IA · 75
Dix, Zachary · 20
Ducommun, Virginia Leonide · 164, 199
Dunavan, Cecilia · 27
Dunn, Sarah · 146

Dupin, Josephine Claudine · 165, 199
Durham, Mary · 17, 27
Durham, Matthew Jr. · 17
Durham, Matthew Sr · 17
Dwigans, Lela A. · 194

E

Eblen, Richard William · 205
Echoes of Ambition · 182
Edwards, Alice Grethel · 193
Edwards, Geneva Blanche · 193
Edwards, John A. · 193
Edwards, Ruby Gertrude · 193
Ehrenberg Pioneer Cemetery · 99
Ehrenberg, Arizona · 99
Elwood Township, Illinois · 25
Emory, John · 60

F

Finley, Adeline · 125
Finley, Amanda Ellen · 125
Finley, Derilda · 125
Finley, George Washington · 125
Finley, James Thomas · 125
Finley, James W. · 125
Finley, Nancy Jane · 125
First Arizona Territorial Legislature · 108
Fletcher, Roy Merriam · 202
Follmann, Clarence W. · 194
Follmann, Clifford Ernest · 194
Follmann, Gladys C. · 194
Follmann, Minnie Marie S. · 193
Follmann, Ralph Francis · 194
Follmann, Roy Bernard · 194
Follmann, William · 194
Fontanelle, Iowa · 152
Fort Laramie Treaty · 186
Fort Whipple, Arizona · 118, 120
Foster, Parker Vorhees Sr. · 198
Fountain Valley, California · 128
Frazier, Elihu · 42
Fuller, Howard Tipton · 202
Funk, Howard · 202

Index

G

Gallagher, John · 129, 166, 201
Galland, Isaac · 34
Garfield, James A. President · 166
Gaylord, Jennett Anna · 128, 166, 201
Gilliam, Verda L. · 195
Gordon Party of 1874 · 186
Gordon, John · 187
Grand River Township, Iowa · 73
Greenfield, Iowa · 141
Guittard, Jeanne Valerie · 203

H

Harper's Bazaar · 180
Harris, Earl · 194
Harris, Ernest · 194
Hartnell Junior College · 154
Hartnell, Marie Teresa · 154, 196
Hartnell, William Edward · 154
Hawkeye Flag · 80
Haworth, Eli · 46, 49
Haworth, Elizabeth Jane · 27
Helbach, Charles A. · 197
Hellyer, Leo D. · 205
Henderson, Mandale J. · 201
Henry, Jane · 18, 146
Heppner, Oregon Flood · 125
Hillger, Vernon R. · 197
Hogan, Albert Dabney · 203
Hogan, Robert · 204
Hogan, Thomas Patrick III · 203
Hogan, Thomas Patrick Jr. · 203
Holaday Seed Company · 154
Holaday, Alfred Chase · 196
Holaday, Almyra Ruth · 192
Holaday, Amy Marie · 193
Holaday, Angeline · 27
Holaday, Anna Mariah · 27
Holaday, Arizona · 102, 206
Holaday, Arthur Stannus · 192
Holaday, Asenath · 27
Holaday, Benjamin Franklin · 197
Holaday, Benjamin Myron · 192
Holaday, Blanche L. · 194

Holaday, Byron C. · 205
Holaday, Caroline · 32, 93, 109, 144, 158, 161, 170, 180, 198
Holaday, Carter Miles · 197
Holaday, Cassius M. · 27
Holaday, Charles Abner · 192
Holaday, Charles Arthur · 194
Holaday, Charles Ernest · 193
Holaday, Clarence · 202, 206
Holaday, Clarence Weinwright · 206
Holaday, Cleo A. · 144, 201
Holaday, Clifford Arthur · 205
Holaday, Clifford Gary · 205
Holaday, Dora · 202
Holaday, Dorothy Irene · 205
Holaday, Elizabeth Ann · 27
Holaday, Ellen · 32, 129, 141, 142, 166, 201
Holaday, Elma Catharine · 194
Holaday, Emma Caroline · 32, 127, 144, 165, 199
Holaday, Ethel · 149, 195
Holaday, Ethel Edna · 202
Holaday, Ethel Elvira · 206
Holaday, Ethel Gertrude · 194
Holaday, Eva M. · 206
Holaday, Florence C. · 157, 198
Holaday, Frances Pearl · 197
Holaday, Gayle B. · 197
Holaday, George · 149
Holaday, George A. · 192
Holaday, George Frederic · 196
Holaday, George Murray · 27
Holaday, George Spies · 204
Holaday, George Washington · 76, 85, 92, 95, 173, 174, 206
Holaday, Gerald Stewart · 193
Holaday, Gertrude · 120, 149, 192
Holaday, Gladys Merle · 205
Holaday, Glenn M. · 195
Holaday, Grover Varel · 205
Holaday, Hannah · 15
Holaday, Harold Rex · 195
Holaday, Harry Miles · 195
Holaday, Helen Bell · 204

Index

Holaday, Helen Lucile · 193
Holaday, Henry Delano · 32, 85, 130, 142, 144, 171, 204
Holaday, Henry George · 205
Holaday, Henry Sr. · 27
Holaday, Howard H. · 195
Holaday, Inez · 27
Holaday, Jacquelyn May · 197
Holaday, James Manton · 196
Holaday, James Perry · 27
Holaday, Jane · 27, 146
Holaday, Jesse · 195
Holaday, John Milton · 32, 43, 93, 127, 144, 155, 197
Holaday, Kenneth Leo, Judge · 196
Holaday, Laurence A. · 193
Holaday, Leo William · 206
Holaday, Leroy C. · 196
Holaday, Lloyd Leslie · 192
Holaday, Lorraine · 197
Holaday, Louisa Bessie · 204
Holaday, Marilyn Ruth · 204
Holaday, Marjorie Lucille · 194
Holaday, Marjorie Marie · 205
Holaday, Mary Ann · 27
Holaday, Mary Joan · 204
Holaday, Mary Spies · 130
Holaday, Maude Ann · 195
Holaday, Mildred Eva · 194
Holaday, Miles · 32, 43, 87, 92, 123, 133, 154, 195
Holaday, Miles Eugene · 154, 196
Holaday, Myra Lydia · 193
Holaday, Nathan Andrew · 154, 196
Holaday, Orpha · 32, 75, 167, 202
Holaday, Pauline · 32, 76, 128, 141, 168, 170, 202
Holaday, Phyllis Layne · 197
Holaday, Robert · 15, 27
Holaday, Roy William · 149, 193
Holaday, Ruth Ann · 27
Holaday, Ruth Elaine · 205
Holaday, Samuel · 13, 27
Holaday, Samuel Meacham · 32, 93, 141, 149, 191
Holaday, Sarah · 25, 27
Holaday, Sidney Earl · 193
Holaday, Thaddeus Samuel · 193
Holaday, Thais Jean · 196
Holaday, Thomas · 27
Holaday, Thomas Jefferson · 32, 70, 167, 202
Holaday, Virginia L. · 195
Holaday, Wallace Earl · 197
Holaday, Wayland Gail · 205
Holaday, Will Tipton · 156, 197
Holaday, William · 15, 16, 27, 128, 141, 144, 166, 201
Holaday, William James · 27
Holaday, William Roy · 194
Holaday, William Thomson · 197
Holaday's Post Office · 73
Holiday, Edward Sidney · 202
Holiday, Robert Samuel · 202
Holiday, Ruth Margaret · 202
Holiday, William · 202
Hollingsworth, Abraham · 146
Hollingsworth, Ada · 147
Hollingsworth, Albert E. · 146
Hollingsworth, Amanda E. · 146
Hollingsworth, America · 146
Hollingsworth, Amos · 146
Hollingsworth, Asberry · 146
Hollingsworth, Berthine · 147
Hollingsworth, Caroline Augusta · 147
Hollingsworth, Charity · 27
Hollingsworth, Charles · 146
Hollingsworth, Clarence · 147
Hollingsworth, Cynthia Ann · 24, 146, 175
Hollingsworth, Cynthia Marcella · 147
Hollingsworth, David Palmer · 147
Hollingsworth, Della Pauline · 147
Hollingsworth, Dorman M. · 147
Hollingsworth, Duane · 147
Hollingsworth, Edwin · 146
Hollingsworth, Elbert · 146
Hollingsworth, Elias · 24, 27, 146, 147
Hollingsworth, Eliza · 24, 146, 147
Hollingsworth, Emily · 146

Index

Hollingsworth, Ezekiel · 18, 22, 25, 29, 34, 39, 51, 146
Hollingsworth, Frances Ellen · 147
Hollingsworth, Frances Jane · 27, 146
Hollingsworth, George · 18, 146
Hollingsworth, George Edwin · 27, 146
Hollingsworth, Henry · 147
Hollingsworth, Ida Belle · 146
Hollingsworth, Jane · 18, 24, 146
Hollingsworth, Jeremiah · 24, 25, 34, 49, 144, 146
Hollingsworth, Jessie · 46
Hollingsworth, John · 24, 25, 27, 146
Hollingsworth, John Wesley · 46, 146
Hollingsworth, Joseph · 18, 146
Hollingsworth, Julia · 146
Hollingsworth, Katherine · 146
Hollingsworth, Landon Miles · 147
Hollingsworth, Livingston · 147
Hollingsworth, Lydia · 24, 25, 29, 31, 34, 67, 76, 85, 92, 138, 141, 142, 145, 155, 191
Hollingsworth, Lydia Letitia · 147
Hollingsworth, Mahundry · 24, 25, 73, 146
Hollingsworth, Margaret · 146
Hollingsworth, Mary · 146
Hollingsworth, Miles · 25, 46, 146
Hollingsworth, Rebecca Jane · 144, 146
Hollingsworth, Ruth Jane · 24, 143, 145, 147, 186
Hollingsworth, Sarah · 22
Hollingsworth, Thomas · 146
Hollingsworth, Valentine · 18, 146
Hollingsworth, Voline · 147
Hollingsworth, William · 24, 144, 146
Hollingsworth, William Dr. · 147
Hollingsworth, Zebulon · 22, 25, 146
Hollywood, California · 164
Holste, Berniece Eleanor · 205
Holste, Joseph John · 205
Hoolbrook, C. Frank · 204
Hoopiiaina, Neely Overland · 197
Hopewell Preparative Meeting · 30
Howard, Anna · 48
Howard, John · 48
Hualapai Indians · 110
Hualapai La Paz Trail of Tears Run · 113

I

Ide's Ranch, California · 59
Iowa Territory · 33

J

Jefferson Township, Iowa · 69, 71, 72
Jenkins, Elizabeth Jean · 197
Jensen, Ivan · 194
Jensen, Margaret Elizabeth · 194
Jessie's Little Book · 46
Johnson, Clara Etta · 195
Johnson, Herbert Hollingsworth · 177
Johnson, Herberta · 178
Johnson, Joseph W. · 177
Johnson, Katherine · 178
Johnson, Lorraine F. · 196
Johnson, Pearl Ann · 195
Johnson, Robert Fielding · 203
Juniper House · 118

K

Kane, Thomas L. · 67
Kanesville · *See* Council Bluffs, Iowa
Karr, Eliza · 146
Kelly, Addie Estella · 27
Kelly, Alpha R. · 27
Kelly, Capron C. · 27
Kelly, Donna Martha · 27
Kelly, Jane Olive · 27
Kelly, Lina Bell · 27
Kelly, Minnie B. · 27
Kelly, Seth · 27
Kelly, Willis · 27
Keokuk County, Iowa · 39, 43, 47, 48, 51
King, Joe · 200

Index

King, Reba Catherine · 205
Kinman, Jennie · 157
Kinman, Mary · 127, 156, 197
Kokomo, Indiana · 24
Krebs, Frances E. · 192

L

Landram, Miles P. · 195
Landram, Samuel Carter · 195
Lannigan, William · 131
Lanteri, Patsy Ann · 205
Larkin claim · 62
Las Bolsas Tract, California · 128
Lee Township, Polk, Iowa · 76
Lick Creek, Indiana · 14
Lieser, Henry Clay · 147
Lieser, Louis · 147
Lindley, Johnathon · 14, 16
Locey, Daniel Moore · 164, 199
Los Cerritos Rancho, California · 129
Lovelace, Ann · 147
Lowe, Enos · 71
Lowry, Margaret Mae · 185, 198

M

Madison County Suffrage Assoc. · 180
Madison County, Iowa · 79
Madisonian · 81
Malone, Carl Curtis · 193
Mann, Frances J. · 92, 123, 154, 195
Markham, Col. Henry H. · 130
Massena, Iowa · 141, 145, 151, 153, 171
Matthews, Edna Ethel · 194
McBride, Gladys Bell · 204
McCool, Walter Deo · 206
McCullough, Kenneth Vernon · 199
McCurdy, Glenn William · 192
McCurdy, Ray Elbert Sr. · 192
McCurdy, Rex Allen · 192
McCurdy, Sidney S. · 192
McCurdy, Van James · 191
McKee, Dolores Lola · 194
McKee, Elnora Irene · 194
McWillie, Janie Pepper · 196

Meacham Graves · 17
Meacham, Dolly · 13, 25, 29, 34, 39, 51, 146
Meacham, George · 17, 27
Meacham, William · 17
Mineral City, Arizona · 99, 110
Mohave City, Arizona · 110
Montezuma Saloon · 119
Montgomery, Alabama · 159
Mount Pleasant Insane Asylum · 160
Mulock, Sarah Paisley · 196
Murray, Benjamin Franklin · 109, 158, 161, 198
Murray, Elizabeth · 144, 160, 170, 177, 180, 199
Murray, Franklin Blair Sr. · 165, 199
Murray, Lenore Kate · 159, 165, 183, 198
Murray, Maude · 159, 163, 198
Murray, Nicholas · 159
Murray, Nicholas William · 160, 199
Murray, Thaddeus S. · 158, 198
Myers, Grace Maud · 192

N

National American Woman Suffrage Assoc. · 180
Nebraska City, Nebraska · 92
Nelson, Alice A. · 196
Newman, Charles James · 180, 199

O

Oakland, California · 168
Oatman, Lorenzo Dow · 98
Oatman, Mary Ann · 98
Oatman, Olive Ann · 98
Ogle, Joe · 200
Oil Queen of Texas · 181
Olive City, Arizona · 98
On the Beauties of Iowa (poem) · 175
Orange County, California · 126
Orlie, Sheriff · 201
Orrick, Mary Francis · 203
Otoe County, Nebraska · 123

Index

P

Palmer, Hester Ann · 147
Panic of 1857 · 76, 80
Patton, Violet · 192
Penn, William · 18
Petersen, Levern V. · 204
Pidgeon, Issac · 39
Pike's Peak · 87, 90
Pine Tree Saloon · 120, 122
Pitcher, Paul · 202
Pitzer House · 80
Pitzer, John A., Judge · 79
Placerville, California · 58
Pleasant Plain, Iowa · 45, 51
Pooler, Carrie Fay · 201
Poore, Irene P. · 197
Prescott, Arizona · 110, 117, 120
Price, Emma Arnette · 199
Pugh, Evan Townsend · 203
Putzier, Flora Helena · 200
Pyles, William Berry Jr. · 197

Q

Quakertown, Indiana · 22

R

Raasch, Thomas August Sr. · 199
Red Rock Line · 44
Revolutionary War · 13
Richland, Iowa · 39, 43, 51
Rizzi, Edith · 201
Robinson Finley, Mary E. · 123, 125, 129, 206
Robinson, Irwin · 125
Rocky Run Cemetery, Iowa · 48
Rocky Run, Iowa · 45, 46, 51
Root, Abner · 152
Root, Almyra · 82, 93, 149, 152, 191
Root, Azariah Jr. · 82, 152
Root, Azariah Sr. · 152
Root, Eli · 153
Root, Martha · 82, 85
Rowe, Joyce L. · 203

Rutt, Abram · 72

S

Sachau, Verdie Valeria · 201
Sacramento, California · 59, 60
Salem, Iowa · 39
Salinas, California · 154
Salmina, Louis William · 196
San Fernando, California · 130
San Francisco, California · 59
San Luis Obispo, California · 133
Saturday Evening Post · 177
Sauk and Fox · 38, 43
Saul, Frank W. · 197
Saurman, Albert B. · 203
Schnellbacher, George H. · 200
Schwaner, Albert Dabney · 170, 203
Schwaner, John Edward · 203
Schwaner, William Frederick Sr. · 203
Schwaner, William Frederick Jr. · 203
Sears, Jean M. · 193
Second Black Hawk purchase · 43
Seulberger, Alice Pauline · 203
Seulberger, Barbara Jane · 203
Seulberger, Julius Carl · 203
Shaver, Robert Andrew · 193
Shaw, Jeanette Lucille · 195
Sheehy, John F. · 204
Shepherd, Carolyn Virginia · 199
Shepherd, Frank Wiley · 181, 199
Sheriff, Orlie James · 201
Shields, Glenn Arthur · 194
Sigourney, Iowa · 50, 51
Singmaster, Mary Ann · 147
Sioux Indians · 187
Skeels, Mariah "Myra" · 152
Slocum, Harold H. · 204
Sonoma County, California · 123
South Dakota · 186
South, Wilber Gerald · 193
Spadra, San Jose Twp, California · 126
Spafford, J. · 60
Spies, Lorraine Deloris · 204
Spies, Mary Averil · 204

Index

Spies, Mary M. · 171, 204
Spies, Varel Everett · 204
Spies, William · 204
St. Joseph, Missouri · 55
St. Nicholas Hotel · 79, 81, 93, 145
Stack, William · 131
Stanford University · 180
Stanton, Samuel · 22
Stearns, Velma Pauline · 192
Stephenson, Mahlon · 51
Stinson, William · 71
Stockwell, Edith Pearl · 195
Stockwell, James Edward Jr. · 196
Stockwell, James Edward Sr. · 195
Stockwell, John Francis Sr. · 196
Stockwell, Lois Esther · 196
Stockwell, Wallace Edward · 195
Stoddard, Dr. · 62, 63, 64
Stoll, William · 157
Stotts, Grethel · 67
Stotts, Unknown · 193
Streb, Alvin Francis · 204
Street, Aaron Jr. · 38
Street, Aaron Mannington · 27
Street, Chastine A. · 27
Street, Cyrus Holaday · 27
Street, Edgar Fremont · 27
Street, Eugene Aaron · 27
Street, Franklin · 27
Street, Hortense Dolly · 27
Street, May Cecelia · 27
Street, Sheridan Dunivan · 27
Street, Willis Franklin · 27
Strong, Rhoda · 125
Studley, Hillary Herbert · 193
Summerhayes, Martha · 100

T

Tabor, Augusta (Pierce) · 91
Tallent, Annie D. · 186
Tarkington, Elizabeth · *See* Murray, Elizabeth
Taylor, Anthony Converse · 164
Taylor, Helen Maurine · 202

Taylor, James Thomas · 201
Taylor, Marjory Louise · 202
Templeton, John · 22
Thompson, Ernest Arkle · 205
Thomson, Gladys Martha · 197
Tingle, Albert Holaday · 27
Tingle, Darcy S. · 27
Tingle, Effie D. · 27
Tingle, John Edward · 27
Tingle, John M. · 27
Tingle, Mary Ellen · 27
Tingle, Samuel C. · 27
Tingle, William Dr. · 27
Tingle, William Oscar · 27
Treaty of 1842 · 43
Trinity River Gold Mines · 59, 135
Tucson, Arizona · 129
Tulare, California · 133
Turley, John H. · 200
Turner, Helen Leticia · 178
Tuscaloosa, Alabama · 159

U

U.S. Deputy Marshal Douglass · 63
Underground Railroad · 12, 16, 39
Union County, Indiana · 18

V

Valentine, Daniel Mulford · 72, 82, 85
Van Horn, Elmer John · 206
Van Horn, Melba Minnie · 206
VanSickle, Francis Marion · 194
Vaughan, Benjamin Franklin · 125
Vermilion Monthly Meeting · 30
Vermilion, Illinois · 16

W

Walden, Emma May · 144
Ward, Murray A. · 163, 199
Ward, Thomas F. · 163, 198
Warren, Mildred R. · 196
Watson, Grady B. · 200
Webber, Rev. Lemuel · 128

Weicker Transfer and Storage Company · 157
Weicker, Eunice Elizabeth · 157, 198
Weicker, Irma Mary · 157, 198
Weicker, Robert Valentine · 157, 198
Weirick, Arthur Murray · 183, 198
Weirick, Emerson Bond · 164, 183, 198
Weirick, Jane Lowry · 185
Weirick, Josephine Frances · 198
Weirick, Maud Helen · 198
Weirick, Thomas Lowry · 185
Welch, Margaret Alvena · 193
Westminster Colony, California · 128
Westward Ho! · 155
Whiskey Row · 119
Whitewater Monthly Meeting · 24
Whitneyville, Iowa · 150, 151
Wickey, Mary · 194
Wilkinson, Bessie Laura · 202
Williams Fork Trail · 108
Willis, Alice M. · 27
Willis, Edward Darwin · 27
Willis, Frank Herbert · 27
Willis, George · 27
Willis, John Milton · 27
Willis, Mary Elizabeth · 27

Willis, Walter John · 27
Winterset Equal Suffrage Association. · 158
Winterset, Iowa · 79
Witcher, Elizabeth Ellen · 147
Witcher, Ephraim · 147, 186
Witcher, Esther Hollingsworth · 189
Witcher, Henry Clay · 147
Witcher, John Frank · 147
Witcher, Kate Alice · 147
Witcher, Martha Jane · 147
Witcher, Nathaniel Edgar · 147
Witcher, Nathaniel Lovelace · 147, 186
Witcher, Winifred · 147
Wolf, Nancy Alice · 146
Woodgrift, Leona · 192
Woolsey, King S. · 107
Work, Robert Van Horn · 198
Wright, Margaret · 18

Y

Yarger, Mildred · 194
Yavapai Indians · 117

Z

Zellweger, Emma · 201

ABOUT THE AUTHOR

I am a member of the Daughters of the American Revolution, the Mayflower Society and the Descendants of Valentine Hollingsworth Sr. Society. I am active on Ancestry.com and maintain a website that is chronically under construction at https://www.familytreenut.info. 😊

In my free time, I enjoy writing, researching, working on the family tree and traveling. I am grateful to my family for the support they've given me for my seemingly endless fascination with all things genealogy.

Thank you also to those who have helped knock down a genealogy brick wall here and there, and especially to those who laid the groundwork so many years ago for me to now be able to piece together what I have. I couldn't have done it without you.

Do you have information to add to this book or a future "The Holadays" series book? Do you have a correction, image or story? Would you just like to say hello? 😊 I'd love to hear from you!

Please contact me at: info@tallgrassprairiebooks.com

Please visit the forum to find post-publishing book updates and to post or read other Holaday/Hollingsworth related information and research.

https://bit.ly/GMHoladay

Or scan:

www.ingramcontent.com/pod-product-compliance
Lightning Source LLC
Chambersburg PA
CBHW070742060526
44119CB00070B/112